SOCIAL JUSTICE

SOCIAL JUSTICE

WILLIAM F. DRUMMOND, S.J.

WESTON COLLEGE

WESTON, MASSACHUSETTS

THE BRUCE PUBLISHING COMPANY

MILWAUKEE

IMPRIMI POTEST:

William E. FitzGerald, S.J.
Provincial

NIHIL OBSTAT:

John A. Schulien, S.T.D.
Censor librorum

IMPRIMATUR:

✠ Albert G. Meyer
Archiepiscopus Milwauchiensis

October 5, 1955

Library of Congress Catalog Card Number: 55-12386

Introduction

THE object of the present study of social justice is not controversy. The opinion offered therein on the nature of social justice differs from those commonly held and consequently some contention must appear. But, in as far as possible, this has been restricted to a mere presentation of differences.

The purpose of the present work is the presentation of a theory of social justice derived from an analysis of all that the encyclical, *Quadragesimo Anno,* says about the subject. Too often, it seems, discussions of social justice trail off into an exposition of St. Thomas' teaching in the matter of legal justice, these two, social and legal justice, being assumed to be the same because of the verbal identity of their aims: the common good. The result of this procedure is that it retards an evolution of doctrine which the encyclical seems to encourage.[1]

The method chosen has been followed for two reasons. First, the conclusion as to the nature of social justice drawn from the text of the encyclical suggests tentative lines of solution to problems of ethics and moral theology which admittedly need further development. Second, since *Quadragesimo Anno* is, in its own words,[2] an invitation to return to the Church extended to all who have turned to socialism in despair brought on by social injustice, the encyclical evidently intends that the doctrine of social justice, precisely

[1] Cf. *Quadragesimo Anno,* n. 48.
[2] *Ibid.,* n. 126.

v

as explained here, should have a powerful appeal for all.

In view of this second consideration, the opening section of the present discussion is devoted to a fundamental explanation and a summary integration of the principles of justice introductory to the more technical investigation of the nature of social justice itself.

For this reason, the professional ethician or moralist will perhaps find little stimulation and certainly no new information in the first chapter, which is a synoptic view of scholastic ethics. However, even they may find something of interest in the attempt made there to synthesize the treatise on justice and to unify it about the concept of the dignity of the human person. There is a unity to this treatise, not seldom overlooked, built around the dignity of man as a person. Rights are a sign of this dignity, as Vermeersch points out;[3] and the rights which pertain to any of the species of justice grow from the concept of human dignity. In terms of this dignity must be formulated the juridical relationships not only between individuals but also between individuals and society.

Finally, the objection may be raised that the whole import of Catholic doctrine is not presented in the following pages. Emphasis is placed on the ordinations of nature, of reason, and the natural law, on the personal dignity of man as a rational creature. But little is said of the elevation of man to a supernatural order, of revelation and grace. Even where the adjective "Catholic" is attributed to a doctrine, it is often used to describe doctrines of natural law which are "Catholic" only in the sense of finding in the Church the "home and shelter"[4] where they have lived and been protected.

---

[3] *Quaestiones de Justitia*, p. 3, n. 6.
[4] Heinrich A. Rommen, *The State in Catholic Thought* (St. Louis: B. Herder, 1945), p. 29.

It is a fact that the truths of revelation and faith are necessary for a complete understanding and appreciation of the life of man, both individual and social. The realities, for instance, of redemption by the blood of God-made-man, of participation by grace in the divine nature, of divine sonship, of membership in the Mystical Body of Christ, are all actualities of our existing supernatural dispensation which infinitely increase the value of the individual soul and the solidarity of men, both of which are implications of human personality.

But, while the supernatural order thus provides a new *motivation* for the observance of justice, the order of justice itself remains an institution of natural law. Grace changes the possessors of rights rather than the rights themselves. Nature is supposed, not destroyed, by grace. And therefore, also, the encyclical does not hesitate to present at every point the arguments derived from natural law. It is a presentation which carries this advantage with it, that it meets men with arguments and principles of Catholic teaching which cannot be shrugged off merely on the score of traditional prejudice against the Church, the realization of which may lead those men, too, to seek in the divine claims of the Church a security worthy of their sincerity.

Contents

SOCIAL JUSTICE

Justice and the Human Person

JUSTICE AND EQUALITY

FUNDAMENTAL to the notion of justice is that of equality. St. Thomas' introduction to his discussion of the virtue — (justice) "implies a certain equality, as the name itself proves" — needed no further corroboration than an appeal to popular use.[1] Justice maintains the balance of social relationships, rendering to each his due, preserving the mutual independence of those who make claims in its name.

The evolution of social and political philosophy confirms this native notion. Let political philosophies be as different as you will, they will justify themselves in the court of human opinion as rationales of the order of justice by an appeal to their defense of equality.

"Equality," however, is more than a word. Its nominal inclusion in a political theory gives no assurance of the realization of justice in a corresponding political system. The reality the word represents can be as diverse in different philosophies as is their understanding of the nature of man. And thus, actually, from the same expression, "the equality of all men," have arisen two social systems, violently opposed to each other in appearance, and both opposed in reality to a Christian social order: individualism and collectivism.

Both, despite their profession of realism, are wrong because they neglect reality. Individualism finds its equality in the equal opportunity and independence of all — the equal chance that any poor boy has to rise to the top by competition. Neglected altogether is the very real social character of the independent individual. Collectivism sees only a nature which in the abstract is alike in all, neglecting the only too obvious differences which concrete circumstances must effect.

The opposition between these systems is more apparent than real.[2] In their fundamental principle they are at one in error. That fundamental principle is materialism of one form or another, either of express denial of the spiritual or of indifference to it in the pursuit of tangible material goods. Guided by this false principle, they fall into the extreme errors which result from their separate interpretations of "equality." "Equality" becomes, in fact, "egalitarianism" — "a colorless uniformity,"[3] the fallacious doctrine of equal treatment, which results in a practical denial of justice.

HUMAN EQUALITY IN THE ENCYCLICALS

The Christian concept of justice and society, as evolved in the encyclicals, too, involves the notion of the equality of men. But the Christian concept of equality cannot admit either individualism or collectivism, for it is an equality of "dignity" which excludes the slavery of some or of all.

This dignity of the human person is, according to the encyclicals, the touchstone of social doctrine. In the State, obedience to authority and genuine liberty are reconciled in that true concept of liberty alone "worthy of human beings."[4] In the family, between husband and wife, that "equality of rights . . . must be recognized in those rights which belong to the dignity of the human. . . ."[5] The rights of labor are postulated by this human dignity: "Labor, indeed, as has been well said by our predecessor in his encyclical, is not a mere chattel; the human dignity of the workingman must be recognized in it, and consequently it cannot be bought and sold like any piece of merchandise."[6] Communism is condemned because of its denial of human dignity: "It is therefore according to the dictates of reason that ultimately all material things should be ordained to man as a person. . . . Communism impoverishes human personality by inverting the terms of the relations of man to society."[7]

In what does this dignity of the human person consist? It consists proximately in his nature, ultimately in his eternal destiny. These two — nature and destiny — are intimately related as a consequence of the necessary and immutable wisdom of God. The end is predesigned in the nature and is realized in the fulfillment of nature. The nature of a creature is the intrinsic font of that creature's activity and operation. It is the very being of the creature considered as a source of activity.[8] And since activity begins and is adequately explained only in virtue of an end that is ultimately intended,[9] there must be a lineal nexus between nature and destiny by reason of which any creature is endowed with such a nature as to expedite that creature for the end for which it was created.

"Any craftsman," writes St. Thomas,[10] "intends to give to his work that aptitude which is best, not absolutely, but in view of a definite end. And even if such an aptitude carry some defect with it, the craftsman is not concerned about this. Thus one who makes a saw for cutting will make it of steel to fit it for its work of cutting. He does not consider making it of glass though this would be more beautiful; for beauty of this kind would impede the end intended. So, also, God gives to every natural thing the disposition which is best, not absolutely, but for the purpose of attaining its proper end."

Man's specific nature is defined by the word rational, in which word are expressed the two powers of soul, intelligence and freedom, which distinguish the possessor from the rest of the visible world, and not merely distinguish him, but give him pre-eminence in being, activity, and in destiny.

Pre-eminence in being is expressed in traditional language by the contrast of the words *imago* and *vestigium*.[11] Man, and only man, is made in the image of God; all other creatures of this world are the vestige of God, the result of His creation, but not in themselves the mirror of His spiritual perfection. And that "image of God" resides in man's soul — spiritual, immortal, with its power of intelligence and free will.[12]

The idea behind the expressions *vestigium* and *imago* is this: All being and all perfection is such only by participation and imitation of the absolute being and perfection of God. To forget this would be to neglect the only fixed and rational norm for the estimation of values. Hence, that creature is of greater dignity which more closely resembles the measure of perfection — God; and that creature is of greatest dignity in whose nature alone, while including the perfection of other creatures, is reflected the spiritual nature of God, becoming by that reflection the "image" of God.[13] Such is the dignity of human nature; and it is because of this dignity, according to St. Thomas, that an individual subsisting in a human nature is called a person.[14]

The words person, or personality, then, first of all signify pre-eminence of being, which is found in the rational and therefore spiritual soul of man.

Pre-eminence of activity naturally follows pre-eminence of being. It consists in the complete physical dominion man has over certain of his acts by his free will. Man, for this reason, is an individual in a more complete sense than any other creature. His human acts are "his" in the sense that can only be predicated of acts which find in their agent their responsible principle. By this fact, not only does man receive the special name, "person,"[15] but by it also the doctrine of personality is completed and integrated, in it being contained the connecting link between the elements in which the dignity of the person consist — nature and destiny. Man's destiny is not to be attained by a necessary compulsion of his nature, but by a process of self-determination.

SOURCE OF HUMAN DIGNITY

The notion of personality forces us to seek beyond the temporal order for the purpose which will explain it. And this extra-temporal or eternal destiny is the ultimate source of the dignity of the human person. To this consideration all that has been said before leads.

For, admitting the spiritual nature of man's soul, we admit implicitly that his existence does not end with death. Admitting his evident superiority, because of that spiritual nature, among the rest of the visible works of creation, we are bound to concede that none of these lesser creatures can be the end toward which he is directed. Such a subordination would be a denial of the intelligence of the Creator.

Or, to express this same truth in another way: the will of man has an innate and necessary tendency to good without limit, but there cannot be found among created goods one which will satisfy that tendency. For all, by the fact of creation, are limited. Yet, there must be some object which in the designs of God is destined to answer to the full the capacity of man's nature.

We are forced, then, to look beyond time for an object,

the possession of which will bring to fruition the personality of man of which we speak. That object is the infinite Good, God, who alone is Truth and Goodness without limit.

It is here that Christian ethics properly takes its start, in God, as the end toward the attaining of which the actions of men must be directed. Thus Pope Pius XI, in his encyclical letter "Divini Redemptoris," setting forth the doctrine of the Church in contrast with that of atheistic communism begins:

> Above all other reality there exists one supreme Being, God, the omnipotent Creator of all things, the all-wise and just Judge of all men. . . . In the Encyclical on Christian Education we explained the fundamental doctrine concerning man as it may be gathered from reason and Faith. Man has a spiritual and immortal soul. He is a person, marvelously endowed by his creator with gifts of body and mind. He is a true "microcosm" as the ancients said, a world in miniature, with a value far surpassing that of the vast inanimate cosmos. God alone is his last end in this life and the next.[16]

In that sentence, "God alone is his last end in this life and the next," the pre-eminence which the human person enjoys by reason of his destiny among all other things on the face of the earth is expressed.

This extra-temporal destiny of the human person penetrates and transforms the whole course of his temporal life. That man is destined for the attainment of a certain perfection in this life, too, is a truth that few will dispute. But the exclusive insistence on such temporal perfectibility will frustrate any effort to construct a philosophy which can validly defend the dignity of man.

Since the ultimate term of perfection to which man is ordered remains one and the same throughout the totality of his existence, it always remains the key to an adequate explanation of his nature. Time and eternity will differentiate man's subjective state in reference to this ultimate destiny, as possession and striving for possession are distinguished. But, because that term remains the same, there can be no perfection to which man is destined in this life which is not at the same time a means to the attainment of the final extra-temporal destiny which is his.

NATURAL LAW AND THE HUMAN PERSON

Consequently, the power of self-determination which belongs to man's free will is not unrestricted. As such it would be destructive of the purpose of the nature to which it belongs. Man's will has its law, derived from man's nature, discovered and proposed by reason, which places restrictions on its freedom of choice; and man's perfection, as a person, consists in the free and responsible development of the powers of his nature, physical, intellectual, and moral, in accordance with the dictates of his reason.

Phrases used to describe this law are often made to sound odious. "Restriction of freedom of choice," for instance, or, "a law imposed by God," are not infrequently misinterpreted to mean some kind of autocratic denial of liberty — an arbitrary, voluntaristic expression of divine dominion.

This misunderstanding is merely a continuation of the error that ascribes creation itself to a self-seeking action on the part of God. However, just as the original creation of man, the sole sufficient reason of which is the infinite goodness of God, can only be intended by God as a communication of divine goodness to creatures;[17] just as the manifestation of God's goodness, the glory of God, which is the purpose of the created world consists in the communicated perfection of created beings, so, also, the natural law implanted in man's nature is properly understood as reason's manifestation of the way in which that communication is to be continued and brought to its perfection. It looks to the good and utility of man. God is not offended, St. Thomas remarks, except in that we act against our own good.[18]

Man, then, carries about with himself the purpose of his being. It is for his own use, his own perfection, that his nature and its law have been given to him, God's glory being attained through the harmonious providence of God in the personal perfection of man.

> For according to Christian Doctrine, man . . . is placed on earth that . . . he may cultivate and evolve to the full all his faculties to the praise and glory of his Creator; and that by fulfilling faithfully the functions of his trade or other calling he may attain both to temporal and eternal happiness.[19]

According to this Catholic doctrine of personality, every human act is conditioned by the thought of eternity. Each act is an ascending stair by which man rises to God. Trivial actions assume importance, imposing facts become insignificant, as each is valued by the glory that it gives to God.

Every act in every field of life must thus be judged in the light of the moral law. Morality is not restricted; it is coextensive with human activity. The nature of man as a person demands this.

> The moral necessity of attaining the ultimate end circumscribes human actions in the domestic, the political, the economic and the purely religious spheres. More exactly we might say that such a conception transforms all activity into moral activity, and every act into a religious act. . . . God is the rationalizing term of human life; all human means will appear rational or irrational just in so far as they lead man towards the attainment of God.[20]

Pope Leo XIII asserts the same truth and with it he illustrates the intrinsic value of every human person which underlies the essential equality between all men:

For however good and desirable mortal life be, yet it is not the ultimate goal for which we are born, but a road only and a means for perfecting, through knowledge of truth and love of good, the life of the soul. The soul bears the express image and likeness of God, and there resides in it that sovereignty through the medium of which man has been bidden to rule all created nature below him and to make all lands and all seas serve his interests. "Fill the earth and subdue it, and rule over the fishes of the sea and the fowls of the air and all living creatures that move upon the earth." In this respect all men are equal, and there is no difference between rich and poor, between masters and servants, between rulers and subjects; "For there is the same Lord of all." No one may with impunity outrage the dignity of man, which God himself treats with great reverence, nor impede his course to that level of perfection which accords with eternal life in heaven. . . .[21]

These words give expression to that quality which epitomizes the dignity of human personality, and which is the root of moral rights about which the social system is built: inviolability. Man, by the fact that he is a man — a rational and free being destined for eternal beatitude in the possession of God — by the fact, in the other words, that he is a "person," can never be a mere means to any created good, either individual or collective. Every man and only man is in this sense sovereign in the world. Each human being enjoys an objective independence, a value which is intrinsic and absolute, not merely extrinsic and relative. Man was not made to be used; he was made for the possession of God forever. That is what the inviolability of a "person" means.

RIGHTS AND THE HUMAN PERSON

It is on this "equality" — the equal dignity of human personality found in every man — that the order of justice and its rights is based. From the independence and sovereignty implied in personality, the notion of natural right is derived. "Rights" protect the inviolability of the person. A natural right is the inviolable power derived from the natural law of possessing or claiming what is "one's own." It is the power, given to the human person by the natural law, of using, without interference, those means which are necessary for the fulfillment of his obligations and for the consequent attainment of his temporal and eternal perfection.

The natural rights thus derived are inviolable in view of the purpose for which they are given; but this does not mean that they are without limit or qualification. The same considerations from which they are derived — the precepts of the natural law and the protection of personality — also determine their respective limitations. There is a hierarchy of goods to which man as a person is destined by the natural order, and, consequently, there is a hierarchy of obligations and of rights, by reason of which some will take precedence over others in cases of apparent conflict.[22] The good of the temporal order is subordinate to his eternal good; the intellectual and physical goods which are his within the temporal order itself are subjected to his moral good — to virtue. These subordinate goods are but means to those to which they are subjected.

Again, another evident limitation of rights arises from the fact that *all* men possess natural rights. The concept of human rights immediately places man in relations with other men. Right, being a moral power, supposes a correlative duty. Justice, the virtue of which rights are the object, is essentially a relative term.[23] It is the virtue by which one is disposed to give another "his due." Thus, the equality of human personality, while conferring on every person equal natural rights, immediately defines and restricts the extent and range of those rights. For, corresponding to every right there is an obligation in others not to infringe upon it: equal rights mean limited rights.

But man has other obligations from nature toward his fellow men besides that of not violating individual rights. He has a positive obligation of working with others for the common good of all. He is by nature a social being. And, therefore, his rights cannot be determined merely by looking at man as an individual. He must be considered in all the relationships that affect him. Rights which an absolute individual would have, are curtailed by the obligations which an individual living in society perceives in that relationship. It is the neglect or distortion of this truth which leads to individualism or collectivism. To avoid these errors certain distinctions must be kept in mind.

The order between individual and society is not the same as that which holds between the temporal good of the individual and his eternal good. In the latter case, the temporal good is subjected to the eternal as means to end, and the common temporal good of society shares this subjection. This follows from the transcendent dignity which is found in the individual person. The relation of the individual to society is not that of means to end, but of a personal member to an organic whole.

> Society is for man, not man for society. This must not be understood in the sense of liberalistic individualism, which subordinates society to the selfish use of the individual; but only in the sense that by means of an organic union with society and by mutual collaboration the attainment of earthly welfare is placed within the reach of all. Further, it is society which affords the opportunities for the development of all the individual and social gifts bestowed on human nature. These natural gifts have a value surpassing the immediate interests of the moment, for in society they reflect the divine perfection, which would not be true were man to live alone. But on final analysis, even in this latter function society is made for man, that he may recognize this reflection of

God's perfection, and refer it in praise and adoration to the Creator. Only man and not society in any form is endowed with reason and a free will subject to the moral law.[24]

Yet the common good, which is the end for which society exists, does take precedence over individual good. And it takes precedence in the sense in which it is a greater good prescribed by the natural law even as the individual good is prescribed. In other words, man is a social being as well as an individual, and as such is susceptible of social obligations which will modify his freedom of action. By virtue of the natural law, society, as well as individual persons, can make "claims" in the name of justice.

PERSON AND SOCIETY

It is at the instigation of nature that man enters into society. Physically and psychologically he is adapted to social life. He is, moreover, morally necessitated to seek in his fellow men the assistance without which he cannot come to a full realization of the potentialities that are his. Of himself he cannot be adequately protected in the enjoyment of his natural gifts; he cannot procure the necessary means for the full development of his physical, intellectual, and moral life. It is in society, and only in society, that man can become the king of creation.

This same truth is stated by Pope Leo XIII:

Man's natural instinct moves him to live in civil society, for he cannot, if dwelling apart, provide himself with the necessary requirements of life, nor procure the means of developing his mental and moral faculties. Hence it is divinely ordained that he should lead his life, — be it family, social or civil, — with his fellow men, amongst whom alone his several wants can be adequately supplied.[25]

The natural end or purpose of society thus formed can

be gathered from this natural necessity which brings society into being. It is to complement by concerted activity the individual efforts of the members in pursuance of their temporal welfare. That means the attaining of those external conditions in which each member may live a life of virtue.

The good of society, then, is a temporal good, an external good, a good common to all — to be shared in by all — and to be attained through the common efforts of all who make up society, complementing individual need. That good is expressed in the words "public peace and prosperity."

Such being its nature, its relation to the personal end of the individual members is clear. Being temporal, it is subordinate to that personal end which is eternal; being external, it is subordinate to the internal good of virtue; being common to all, it is to be acquired by the combined efforts of all; it subordinates to itself individual good of the same order,[26] external and temporal, yet is subordinate in this same order to the individual good of all the members taken together.

That all should strive for this common end in society, a co-ordinating principle of effective direction is necessary. This principle is authority. And even as society itself is prescribed by God through nature, so through nature He gives to society this necessary property, without which it could not attain its natural end. "(But) as no society can hold together unless someone be over all, directing all to strive earnestly for the common good, every civilized community must have a ruling authority, and this authority, no less than society itself, has its source in nature, and has consequently God for its author. Hence it follows that all public power must proceed from God...."[27]

The limits of this authority in society are defined by the end for which it is given by nature. In general, it can be said to extend to everything that is required by the com-

mon good.[28] Evidently it cannot contradict the natural law
from which it is derived; it cannot command what is in-
trinsically evil; but it can prohibit an act, which though
good in itself, would in concrete circumstances be against
the common good.[29]

When human authority so limits or determines activity,
it can only do so in the interest of the common good, in
virtue of the natural law, which prescribes that the extent
and condition of the exercise of rights left indeterminate
by it should be made determinate by that authority it provides for the purpose of welding and harmonizing individuals in their quest for the common good.

In this case the true good of the individual is not neglected, nor is violence done to his personality. For the true
good of the individual, and the perfection of his personality
consists, as has been said, in the observance of the natural
law which imposes duties, social as well as individual.

Thus, in the matter of private property:

> It follows from the twofold character of ownership which,
> as we have said, is both individual and social, that men
> must take into account in this matter, not only their own
> advantage, but also the common good. To define in detail
> these duties, when need occurs, and when the natural law
> does not do so, is the function of the civil ruler. Provided that
> the natural and divine law be observed, the public authority,
> in view of the true necessities of the common welfare, may
> specify more accurately what is licit and illicit for property
> owners in the use of their possessions. . . .[30]

Clearly in matters of this nature, practical cases are often
of such difficulty and complexity that human reason can
easily err. It is clear, too, that the pretext of the common
good will "de facto" be used by the exponents of collective
materialism to suppress the dignity of the individual. But
the principle which "de jure" regulates the relation of
public authority to individual rights is clear: It can never

take them away; it can only regulate their use, and that, only when the common good demands such regulation.

> From the pre-eminence — of the common good over the particular good of individuals, it does not follow that society has the right to dictate the law to its members arbitrarily and to dispose, according to its good pleasure, of their rights and their liberty. The just limits of the jurisdiction of authority are fixed by the exigencies of the common good. Now inasmuch as the common good has no reason for existence other than to aid the members in the fulfilment of their personal destinies and to compensate for their natural deficiency, it follows that, in every case where their personal initiatives, isolated or spontaneously united, are sufficient for the realization of this task, collective help and the intervention of social authority become superfluous, nay harmful. . . .[31]

DIVISIONS OF JUSTICE

There is thus, based on the nature of man, a network of social relationships in which the meaning of "one's due" is verified in a threefold way. The individual as a human person has an intangible province of self-direction by reason of which he enjoys inviolable claims to those goods without which self-realization would be impossible; the state has a claim to those acts of its members which are necessary for the attainment of its God-given end, the common good; and because this good must flow back into the good of the members, the members of the state as such have a claim to participation in the full life of the whole.

Thus men are bound together as individuals and as members of society in virtue of the natural law, by triple bonds of justice. Commutative justice is the link between individual and individual.[32] In virtue of it each is bound to give to the other the goods which nature has destined for him as an individual: life, liberty, and the pursuit of happiness, with all that they imply. Legal justice and distributive justice are the bonds between the individual and the community: the first obliging all to strive for the common good according to their several abilities;[33] the second governing and regulating the proportionate distribution of common social burdens and benefits.[34]

Beyond this classic threefold division of justice, another (at least, nominally different) division has been prominent in social discussions and documents from rather recent times: social justice.

NOTES FOR CHAPTER ONE

1. *Summa Theologica*, II–II, q. 57, a. 1.
2. Cf. Amintore Fanfani, *Catholicism, Protestantism and Capitalism* (New York: Sheed and Ward, 1939), pp. 92–93.
3. *Pius XII and Democracy*, Christmas Message, 1944 (Paulist Press), n. 33.
4. *Immortale Dei*, encyclical of Leo XIII on the Christian Constitution of States, 1885 (trans., *Catholic Mind*, Nov. 8, 1936), p. 443.
5. *Casti Connubii*, encyclical of Pius XI on Christian Marriage, 1931 (trans., *Catholic Mind*, Jan. 22, 1931), p. 44.
6. *Quadragesimo Anno*, encyclical of Pius XI on the Reconstruction of Social Order, 1931 (trans., N.C.W.C., 1942), n. 83.
7. *Divini Redemptoris*, encyclical of Pius XI on Atheistic Communism, 1937 (Vatican: Polyglot Press, 1937), n. 30.
8. *Summa Theol.* I, q. 29, a. 4, ad 4.
9. *Summa Contra Gentiles*, III, c. 17.
10. *Summa Theol.* I, q. 91, a. 3.
11. *Ibid.* I, q. 93, a. 1 and a. 2.
12. *Ibid.* I, q. 93, a. 6.
13. *Ibid.* I, q. 93, a. 2, c.
14. *Ibid.* I, q. 29, a. 3, ad 2.
15. *Ibid.* I, q. 29, a. 1, c.
16. Nn. 26 and 27.
17. *Summa Theol.* I, q. 44, a. 4.
18. *Contra Gentiles*, III, c. 122.
19. *Quad. Anno*, n. 118.
20. Fanfani, *op. cit.*, p. 122.
21. *Rerum Novarum*, encyclical of Leo XIII on the Condition of Labor, 1891 (N.C.W.C., 1942), n. 57.
22. J. Messner, *Social Ethics* (St. Louis: Herder, 1949), p. 22 ff.
23. *Summa Theol.*, II–II, q. 57, a. 1, c; q. 58, a. 1 and a. 2.
24. *Divini Redemptoris*, n. 29.
25. *Immortale Dei*, p. 426.
26. *Summa Theol.*, II–II, q. 152, a. 4, ad 3.
27. *Immortale Dei*, loc. cit.
28. Suarez, *De Legibus*, Bk. III, Chap. XII, nn. 8, 9, 10.

29. *Ibid.*, n. 19.
30. *Quad. Anno*, n. 49.
31. "Person and Society," *Race: Nation: Person,* ed. Corrigan and O'Toole (New York: Barnes and Noble, 1944), p. 235.
32. *Summa Theol.*, II–II, q. 61, a. 1, c.
33. *Ibid.*, ad 4; q. 58, a. 5 and a. 6.
34. *Ibid.*, q. 61, a. 1.

CHAPTER ONE
STUDY AIDS

Review Questions:

How are the notions "equality" and "justice" related?

Does human equality imply that all men should be treated in exactly the same way?

Have communism and individualism anything in common?

What is the special implication of the word "person"?

What is the true foundation of the dignity of man?

What is the effect of an eternal destiny on the temporal life of man?

In what does the true perfection of man consist?

What is the natural law?

Are the restrictions of freedom which come from the natural law irrational?

Does the natural law arise from the whim of God?

Is the moral law for man's benefit? How?

What is meant by the inviolability of the human person?

What is meant by a natural right?

What is the connection between human inviolability and natural rights?

Are human rights limited?

Is it intended by the natural law that man should live in society?

Is the human person merely a part of society?

Does society, as well as individual man, possess rights?

Is there any conflict between these rights?

What is the purpose for which society exists?

What is the relation between the individual good of man and the common good of society?

Is authority necessary in society?

Whence does authority come?

Is social authority limited? What are some of these limitations?

What are the principal divisions of justice?

Discussion Topics:

The decline of individualism in the United States.

Differences between a doctrine of "equality" and that of "egalitarianism."

The influence of religion on the recognition of the dignity of man.

Historical changes in the meaning of liberalism.

Moral law and economic law.

Suggested Readings:[1]

Cahill, E., S.J., *The Framework of a Christian State* (Dublin: M. H. Gill and Son, 1932), Chap. XVI.

Cronan, E. P., *The Dignity of the Human Person* (New York: Philosophical Library, 1955), Chaps. 3 and 4.

Cronin, J. F., S.S., *Catholic Social Principles,* Chaps. III, IV, V.

Divine, T. F., S.J., "On the Assumption of 'Rational Conduct' in Economic Science," *Review of Social Economy,* Vol. VIII (Sept., 1950), pp. 85–88.

Farrell, W., O.P., *A Companion to the Summa* (New York: Sheed and Ward, 1938), Vol. II, Chap. XXI.

Higgins, George G., "After Sixty Years," *Social Order,* May, 1951, pp. 195–204.

Hughes, E. J., *The Church and the Liberal Society* (New Jersey: Princeton Univ. Press, 1944), pp. 3–51.

Killeen, E. C., O.Praem., "Ethics, Data for the Economist," *Review of Social Economy,* Vol. VII (Mar., 1949), pp. 8–21.

Maritain, J., *Man and the State,* Chap. IV.

McKeon, R. M., S.J., "New Capitalism Vs. Old," *Social Order,* Mar., 1953, pp. 99–102.

Neill, T. P., "Liberalism," *Social Order,* Oct., 1954, pp. 339–346.

Sheed, F. J., *Communism and Man* (Sheed and Ward, 1938), pp. 160–184.

---

[1] In the "Suggested Readings" appended to each chapter, complete information is given only on those works which are not included in the general bibliography.

Social Justice and the Encyclicals

THE DISPUTED MEANING OF SOCIAL JUSTICE

THE number of opinions with regard to the nature of social justice is legion. They range all the way from the conception of social justice as a vague term descriptive of the general well-being of the social body to the affirmation of social justice as a new and distinct species of the virtue of justice in the strict sense. In the positions between these extremes, it is variously made out to be a harmonious balance of the three traditional types of justice, or it is equivalated to a combination of distributive and legal justice, or it is identified with one or the other of these two.

It is not the intention of the present inquiry to end these disputes about the nature of social justice. Social justice is a concept still evolving as the whole modern social complex where justice must be applied is evolving. And in this evolution each opinion on the nature of the virtue helps, by discussion, to clarify the concept which holds such a prominent place in modern papal teaching.[1]

Nevertheless, it seems that any discussion of the subject may fairly start with the supposition that it is from the texts of the encyclicals *Rerum Novarum* and *Quadragesimo Anno,* and particularly from the latter, that the exact meaning of "social justice" in Catholic social teaching is to be determined. With very good reason Ferree[2] points out that, "The only reasonable place to study either notion (Catholic Action or social justice) is in the work of Pius XI and in works inspired by his teaching; for it is only here that the words are surely used with a definite and precise signification."

And of the works of Pius XI, it is the encyclical *Quadragesimo Anno* which should be considered as definitive in the matter. For in this encyclical "social justice" is not used merely in passing, but is proposed as the specific remedy for the precise evils and disorders to which the letter is devoted. The reform sought by *Quadragesimo Anno* is to be attained by a complete moral renovation but particularly and peculiarly by the observance of "social justice," as is stated explicitly by the Holy Father who affirms his purpose of "striving to restore society according to the mind of the Church on the firmly established basis of *social justice* and social charity."[3]

The encyclical *Rerum Novarum,* though it does not use the term "social justice," must be considered, at least briefly, as giving the background for *Quadragesimo Anno,* as will be apparent immediately. An examination of these encyclicals indicates first of all that "social justice" is a form of justice concerned with the socioeconomic order.

SOCIAL JUSTICE AND THE ECONOMIC ORDER

A "social reform" can take on many aspects. It can refer to any one of man's multiple social institutions: to the family and domestic society; to the state and civil society. It can be concerned with any of man's social activities: educational, cultural, recreational, political. That *Quadragesimo Anno* and *Rerum Novarum* are concerned with the economic order and that therefore "social justice" in its strict sense finds its application within this order is evidenced by a consideration of both the general tenor of the encyclicals and the particular passages in which the term "social justice" is used.

Considered in a general way, it seems that the encyclicals take pains to restrict themselves to the field of economic life. In its division of matter[4] *Quadragesimo Anno* gives as its purpose: to defend and develop the teaching of Leo XIII on the social and economic question as proposed in the encyclical *Rerum Novarum,* and to summon to court the present economic regime.

Leo XIII, whose doctrine is to be defended and developed, announces in the opening paragraphs of *Rerum Novarum* the occasion of its writing: the conflict in the *field of economics.* Admitted is the disturbance in the political sphere; admitted, too, is the oneness of source of all current social conflict; the spirit of revolutionary change. But it is the impact of this spirit on the economic order which occasions the encyclical. New developments in industry, new techniques, new relations of employer and employee, the abounding wealth of a few as contrasted with the destitution of the masses, the closer bond of union among workers — all causes of conflict in the socioeconomic order are to be treated in *Rerum Novarum.*

It is therefore the set purpose of the encyclical[5] to treat of the "Condition of the Workers," not as this question would be treated incidentally in a letter on liberty, civil authority, or any other related subject, but precisely that the conflict involved may be resolved. The problem facing Leo XIII was that of the workers defenseless against the inhumanity of employers and the greed of competitors, of the yoke almost of slavery laid on the masses of nonowning workers by a very few rich men.[6] And therefore the rights and duties to be treated are those of the economic order: of capital and labor, of rich and poor.[7]

The same restricting concern with the economic order marks the introduction of *Quadragesimo Anno.* Other problems — social problems — have been the subject matter of other encyclicals: problems of the family, of civil authority, of the duties of Catholics as citizens, of socialism, of human liberty. *Rerum Novarum,* however, took as its subject matter the difficult "Social Question,"[8] a question which arose as a result of a new kind of economic life and new developments in industry.[9] It is the question of want in the midst of plenty; the question of the division of human society into classes, one small in number enjoying all the benefits of wealth, the other embracing the great multitude of working people oppressed by poverty. It is an economic state of affairs which those who enjoyed the abundance of riches looked upon as the result of "inevitable economic laws."[10]

Consequently, too, those who with one voice begged that a safe road in this conflict be pointed out by the Supreme Pontiff were those who "ex professo" were concerned with the economic order: "men well versed in social questions, employers and workers themselves."[11]

Supporting this contention that the encyclicals *Quadragesimo Anno* and *Rerum Novarum* are precisely concerned with the reformation of the economic order is the passage from *Divini Redemptoris*:[12]

> If, therefore, we consider the whole structure of *economic life,* as we have already pointed out in our encyclical Quadragesimo Anno, the reign of justice and charity in *social-economic relations* can only be achieved when professional and interprofessional organizations, based on the solid foundations of Christian teaching, constitute, under forms adapted to different places and circumstances, what used to be called guilds.

PARTICULAR PASSAGES IN "QUADRAGESIMO ANNO"

Descending now from the general consideration of the encyclical to an examination of the particular passages of *Quadragesimo Anno* in which the term "social justice" is used, we find the same conclusion borne out: "Social justice" is always proposed as the fundamental guiding principal for the solution of *economic* questions.

The term first appears in the encyclical in numbers 57 and 58 in the midst of the discussion on the relationship between capital and labor. More specifically, the subject matter of these paragraphs is that of the distribution of property and wealth, of the "riches that social economic developments constantly increase." The demand of social justice is such a distribution of this wealth that the "common good of all society will be kept inviolate."

But not every distribution among human beings of property and wealth is of a character to attain either completely or to a satisfactory degree of perfection the end which God intends. Therefore the riches that economic-social developments constantly increase ought to be so distributed among individual persons and classes that the common advantage of all, which Leo XIII had praised, will be safeguarded; in other words, that the common good of all society will be kept inviolate. By this law of social justice, one class is forbidden to exclude the other from sharing in the benefits. Hence the class of the wealthy violates this law no less, when, as if free from care on account of its wealth, it thinks it the right order of things for it to get everything and the worker nothing, than does the non-owning working class when, angered deeply at outraged justice and too ready to assert wrongly the one right it is conscious of, it demands for itself everything as if produced by its own hands, and attacks and seeks to abolish therefore, all property and returns or incomes, of whatever kind they are or whatever the function they perform in human society, that have not been obtained by labor, and for no other reason save that they are of such a nature. And in this connection we must not pass over the unwarranted and unmerited appeal made by some to the Apostle when he said: "If any man will not work neither let him eat." For the Apostle is passing judgment on those who are unwilling to work, although they can and ought to, and he admonishes us that we ought diligently to use our time and energies of body and mind and not be a burden to

others when we can provide for ourselves. But the Apostle
in no wise teaches that labor is the sole title to a living or
an income.

To each, therefore, must be given his own share of goods,
and the distribution of created goods, which, as every discerning person knows, is laboring today under the gravest
evils due to the huge disparity between the few exceedingly
rich and the unnumbered propertyless, must be effectively
called back to and brought into conformity with the norms
of the common good, that is, social justice.[13]

SOCIAL JUSTICE AND THE COMMON GOOD

Here (as in other places) the common good is indicated
as the end of social justice. Led by this fact, not a few authors
have concluded that therefore social justice is but another
name for legal justice. A closer consideration of the meaning
of "common good" in the context, however, makes such
easy identification very doubtful. The common good here
spoken of, in so far as it is the end of "social justice," is not
that *complete* order of society in which every member enjoys
the possibility of realizing his true self.[14] It does not com-
prehend all those values of human life such as peace, freedom, cultural opportunities which the end of legal justice
includes. It is given a restricted meaning: the common good
of the economic order — the common good which comes
from such a division of wealth that all may share in the
benefits of the socioeconomic process.

And therefore, also, the subjects of this virtue are not men
as citizens but men as members of the economic order — the
two groups, capital and labor, with whom the whole section
is concerned. Violators of the "law of social justice" are all
those who would impede others from sharing in the benefit
of economic development: The wealthy who claim everything for themselves; the outraged non-owning workers who
demand that everything should go to labor alone.

It is the demand of "social justice" that there be such a distribution of economic goods that the vast differences between the wealthy and the destitute — an *economic* condition which threatens society — may be eliminated.

SOCIAL JUSTICE AND WAGES

The practical means, indicated by the encyclical, of effecting this redistribution of good and desired spread of ownership is not any revolutionary disappropriation, but an evolutionary reformation of the existing wage system. And it is in this connection that the next appeal in the name of "social justice" is made.[15] Again it is an economic problem.

In this question of wages, however, social justice does not immediately regulate the contract between individual employer and employee. That is a matter of "natural" justice,[16] of giving the laborer the strict worth of his hire,[17] of the "strictest justice — commutative justice, as it is called."[18] A living, family wage is thus due to the worker.

Social justice is to regulate the economic order as a whole. It looks to the common good, but again of the *economic* order, so regulating that order that all may be able to obtain from it a family wage. Social justice demands that economic conditions be so adjusted that businesses will be able to pay workers that family wage which is due in strict justice.

In the first place, the worker must be paid a wage sufficient to support him and his family. That the rest of the family should also contribute to the common support, according to the capacity of each, is certainly right, as can be observed especially in the families of farmers, but also in the families of many craftsmen and small shop keepers. But to abuse the years of childhood and the limited strength of women is grossly wrong. Mothers, concentrating on household duties, should work primarily in the home or in its immediate vicinity. It is an intolerable abuse, and to be abolished at all cost, for mothers on account of the father's low wage to be forced to engage in gainful occupations outside the home to the neglect of their proper cares and duties, especially the training of children. Every effort must therefore be made that fathers of families receive a wage large enough to meet ordinary family needs adequately. But if this cannot always be done under existing circumstances, social justice demands that changes be introduced as soon as possible whereby such a wage will be assured to every adult workingman. It will not be out of place here to render merited praise to all, who with a wise and useful purpose, have tried and tested various ways of adjusting the pay for work to family burdens in such a way that, as these increase, the former may be raised and indeed, if the contingency arises, there may be enough to meet extraordinary needs.[19]

This same regulative character of social justice is again indicated at the end of this discussion on wages. Here the final qualification of a just wage is laid down: It should be what may be called a "maximum employment" wage — a wage, that is, which admits the widest possible opportunity to work. This is a demand of social justice.

Lastly, the amount of the pay must be adjusted to the public economic good. We have shown above how much it helps the common good for workers and other employees, by setting aside some part of their income which remains after necessary expenditures, to attain gradually to the possession of a moderate amount of wealth. But another point, scarcely less important, and especially vital in our times, must not be overlooked: namely, that the opportunity to work be provided to those who are able and willing to work. This opportunity depends largely on the wage and salary rate, which can help as long as it is kept within proper limits, but which on the other hand can be an obstacle if it exceeds these limits. For everyone knows that an excessive lowering of wages, or their increase beyond due measure, causes unemployment. This evil, indeed, especially as we see it prolonged and injuring so many during the years of Our Pontificate, has plunged workers into misery and temptations, ruined the prosperity of nations, and put in jeopardy the public order, peace, and tranquility of the whole world. Hence it is contrary to social justice when, for the sake of personal gain and without regard for the common good, wages and salaries are excessively lowered or raised; and this same social justice demands that wages and salaries be so managed, through agreement of plans and wills, in so far as can be done, as to offer to the greatest possible number the opportunity of getting work and obtaining suitable means of livelihood.[20]

The encyclical could hardly be more explicit in making the demands of social justice, demands of the economic order. As before, the common good is the purpose of social justice. But, again, this "common good" is the *economic* common good. The expression, "common good," used in the concluding sentence of this paragraph is quite clearly resumptive of the expression "public economic good" which occurs in the introductory sentence. There is an evident parallel between both sentences: the first enunciates the principle that the wage rate must be adjusted to the common good; the last, after pointing out that unemployment is the economic result of an exclusive application of either a purchasing power theory or a cost theory of wages, applies the principle. The common good in either case is the same: the public *economic* good. And, the logical consequence of the preceding is that "social justice" demands that wages and salaries be so managed through agreement of plans and wills, in so far as can be done, as to offer to the greatest possible number the opportunity of getting work and obtaining suitable means of livelihood — a demand of the economic order.

SOCIAL JUSTICE THE DIRECTING PRINCIPLE OF ECONOMIC LIFE

Two things especially are necessary for the realization of the papal program: a reform of institutions and a correction of morals.[21] The latter, treated fully in the closing paragraphs[22] of the encyclical, is shown to be indispensable to the former. For the reconstruction of social order is envisaged in the encyclicals as a result of the application of moral principles; it depends on the acceptance on the part of all concerned of the solidarity of all men. Most destructive of the unity desired is the free competition which individualism has accepted as the guiding principle of economic life. And therefore in its place "a true and effective directing principle" which will govern the reconstituted social-economic order must be introduced. That principle again is social justice.

> Attention must be given also to another matter that is closely connected with the foregoing. Just as the unity of human society cannot be founded on an opposition of classes, so also the right ordering of economic life cannot be left to a free competition of forces. For from this source, as from a poisoned spring, have originated and spread all the errors of individualist economic teaching. Destroying through forgetfulness or ignorance the social and moral character of economic life, it held that economic life must be considered and treated as altogether free from and independent of public authority, because in the market, i.e., in the free struggle of competitors, it would have a principle of self-direction which governs it much more perfectly than would the intervention of any created intellect. But free competition, while justified and certainly useful provided it is kept within certain limits, clearly cannot direct economic life — a truth which the outcome of the application in practice of the tenets of this evil individualistic spirit has more than sufficiently demonstrated. Therefore, it is most necessary that economic life be again subjected to and governed by a true and effective directing principle. This function is one that the economic dictatorship which has recently displaced free competition can still less perform, since it is a headstrong power and a violent energy that, to benefit people, needs to be strongly curbed and wisely ruled. But it cannot curb and rule itself. Loftier and nobler principles — social justice

and social charity — must, therefore, be sought whereby this dictatorship may be governed firmly and fully. Hence the institutions themselves of people and, particularly those of all social life, ought to be penetrated with this justice, and it is most necessary that it be truly effective, that is, establish a juridical and social order which will, as it were, give form and shape to all economic life. Social charity, moreover, ought to be as the soul of this order, an order which public authority ought to be ever ready effectively to protect and defend. It will be able to do this the more easily as it rids itself of those burdens which, as We have stated above, are not properly its own.[23]

Here the relationship of social justice to the economic order is patent. The whole section is concerned with the restoration of the directing principle of economic life. That principle as contrasted with unlimited free competition and economic dictatorship (which has succeeded competition) is social justice and social charity.

The result, moreover, of the infusion of this justice into all the institutions of social life will be to give form and shape to *"all economic life."* In other words, *as far as this encyclical is concerned,* the purpose of the reformation of any public institutions, of the whole juridical and social order, is socioeconomic reconstruction. And, therefore, the summary paragraph (n. 90) refers back to the principle which is to inform the reconstituted members of the social order as "the directing principle of *economic* life." That principle is social justice.

This restriction of social justice to the concerns of the economic order does not make the term synonymous with economic justice. As indicated above, in the discussion of wages, commutative justice holds an essential and fundamental place in the relation of worker and employer. Social justice, as the same section indicates, supposes the economic obligations of commutative justice and is regulative of the whole economic order, establishing those conditions in which the demands of commutative justice may be fulfilled for the common good of all concerned.

SOCIAL JUSTICE AND CAPITALISM

It is this end — the common good — which is emphasized in the next two references to social justice. In the first of these (paragraph 101), social justice and the common good are mentioned in the same breath.

> That, in the first place, the whole aspect of economic life is vastly altered, is plain to all. You know, Venerable Brethren and Beloved Children, that the Encyclical of Our Predecessor of happy memory had in view chiefly that economic system, wherein, generally, some provide capital while others provide labor for a joint economic activity. And in a happy phrase he described it thus: "Neither capital can do without labor, nor labor without capital."
>
> With all his energy Leo XIII sought to adjust this economic system according to the norms of right order; hence, it is evident that this system is not to be condemned in itself. And surely it is not of its own nature vicious. But it does violate right order when capital hires workers, that is, the non-owning working class, with a view to and under such terms that it directs business and even the whole economic system according to its own will and advantage, scorning the human dignity of the workers, the social character of economic activity and social justice itself, and the common good.[24]

Here, introducing the discussion of modern capitalism and its evolution since the time of Leo XIII, *Quadragesimo Anno* makes the important distinction between the system of capitalism in itself and the abuses of historic capitalism. The former is not evil; the abuses are scored as violations of right order. It is a question, again, very explicitly, of an economic system and its deordination. Capitalism has violated right order in directing business and economic activity to capital's arbitrary will and advantage, "Scorning the human dignity of the workers, the social character of economic activity and social justice itself, and the common good."

The "common good" here mentioned either means the common *economic* good (which seems at least probable from the context), in which case the proposition stands that social justice is a justice of the economic order, or it means the common good of society in its total amplitude. In this understanding of the term, too, the restriction of "social justice" to the economic order is entirely justified by the text of the encyclical. For the violation of social justice which is against this common good consists precisely in the scorning of "the social character of economic activity."

Again, in paragraph 110, we find this same close association of social justice and the common good. In fact it is because of the wording of this section, together with a passage from *Divini Redemptoris,* which remains to be considered, that many are convinced of the identification of legal, or "common good," justice and social justice. For here "the needs of the common good" are termed "the norm of social justice."

In the second part of this Encyclical where We have presented Our teaching, We have described the remedies for these great evils so explicitly that We consider it sufficient at this point to recall them briefly. Since the present system of economy is founded chiefly upon ownership and labor, the principles of right reason, that is, of Christian social philosophy, must be kept in mind regarding ownership and labor and their association together, and must be put into actual practice. First, so as to avoid the reefs of individualism and collectivism, the two-fold character, that is individual and social, both of capital or ownership and of work or labor must be given due and rightful weight. Relations of one to the other must be made to conform to the laws of strictest justice, commutative justice, as it is called — with the support, however, of Christian charity. Free competition, kept within definite and due limits, and still more economic dictatorship, must be effectively brought under public authority in these matters which pertain to the latter's function. The public institutions themselves, of peoples, moreover, ought to make all human society conform to the needs of the common good; that is, to the norm of social justice. If this is done, that most important division of social life, namely, economic activity, cannot fail likewise to return to right and sound order.[25]

Strong, however, as the identification of legal and social justice appears at firsthand in the foregoing, a closer consideration of the context seems to restrict the common good in question to that of the economic order, and therefore to distinguish, at least inadequately, the two types of justice.

The paragraph is devoted to a review of the remedies already treated at length in previous parts of the encyclical — remedies for the evils, summarized in the preceding paragraph, brought about by the "individualistic spirit in *economic* life." The ultimate and basic remedy here, as elsewhere, is social justice. Furthermore, in the first part of this section, Pope Pius enumerates the areas and elements of the social order to which the remedy of social justice is to be applied. All are of the economic order: ownership; capital and labor, and the relationship between them; free competition and economic dictatorship. In the last sentence of the paragraph, the *one* effect of the application of the norm of social justice singled out is the return of *economic* activity to right and sound order.

SOCIAL JUSTICE IN "DIVINI REDEMPTORIS"

Here, for the sake of emphasizing the point, it seems well to propose the section from the encyclical *Divini Redemptoris* which, like the preceding, appears to identify legal and social justice, declaring that "it is of the very essence of social justice to demand from each individual all that is necessary for the common good." The passage is long, but its citation in full is necessary to put the relationship of social justice to the common good in context.

For, in reality, besides commutative justice, there is also social justice with its own set of obligations, from which neither employers nor working men can escape. Now it is of the very essence of social justice to demand from each individual all that is necessary for the common good. But just as in the living organism it is impossible to provide for the good of the whole unless each single part and each individual member is given what it needs for the exercise of its proper functions, so it is impossible to care for the social organism and the good of society as a whole unless each single part and each individual member — that is to say, each individual man in the dignity of his human personality — is supplied with all that is necessary for the exercise of his social functions. If social justice be satisfied, the result will be an intense activity in economic life as a whole, pursued in tranquility and order. This activity will be proof of the health of the social body, just as the health of the human body is recognized in the undisturbed regularity and perfect efficiency of the whole organism.

But social justice cannot be said to have been satisfied so long as working men are denied a wage that will enable them to secure proper sustenance for themselves and for their families; so long as they are denied the opportunity of acquiring a modest fortune and avoiding the pauperism which is so widespread; so long as they cannot make suitable provision through public or private insurance for old age, for periods of illness and unemployment. In a word, to repeat what has been said in our Encyclical *Quadragesimo Anno:* "Then only will the economic and social order be soundly established and attain its ends, when it offers, to all and to each, all those goods which the wealth and resources of nature, technical science and the social organization of economic affairs can give. These goods should be sufficient to supply all necessities and reasonable comforts, and to uplift men to that higher standard of life which, provided it be used with prudence, is not only not a hindrance but is of singular help to virtue."[26]

In an analysis of these two numbers, several pertinent observations occur. The first sentence, besides clearly distinguishing social justice from commutative justice, singles out particular subjects of the obligations of social justice. They are subjects of the *economic* order: "Social justice with its own set of obligations from which neither employers nor working men can escape."

The end of paragraph 51 gives the result of the satisfying of social justice. It is the tranquil order of *"economic life as a whole,"* which is another way of saying the common economic good.

Paragraph 52 enumerates particular violations of social justice: denial to workingmen of a living family wage; denial of the opportunity of acquiring property; denial of the possibility of insurance for old age, illness, and unemployment. All are violations which pertain to the economic order.

And finally the encyclical *Quadragesimo Anno* is cited to clinch the point intended in this section. The quotation calls for such an ordering of *economic* life that to all and each it offers all those goods which are necessary for a life of virtue.

Such a congeries, occurring in this key passage, can scarcely be accidental. The subjects of the virtue, the violations of the virtue, the effects of the virtue, as enumerated by the encyclical, are all of the economic order. This, taken in conjunction with the constant explicit association of social justice with economic life throughout the encyclical *Quadragesimo Anno,* seems to justify the statement that, in the intention of Pope Pius XI, social justice is concerned with the economic order, and the "common good" indicated as the end of social justice is the common *economic* good.

THE BASIS OF ECONOMIC REFORM

Returning now to the encyclical *Quadragesimo Anno* and

its last reference to social justice, we must revert to the consideration of the general scope of the encyclicals to determine the meaning of the term. This section[27] invites those who have deserted to the camp of socialism to return to the church, "where their own place is, in the ranks of those who, zealously following the admonitions which Leo promulgated and We have solemnly repeated, are striving to restore society to the mind of the church, on the firmly established basis of *Social Justice* and Social Charity."

Considered in view of the general tenor of the encyclical, this unadorned mention of social justice is strongly confirmatory of all that has thus far been said of the nature of the virtue. For here social justice is unambiguously stated to be the basis of that restoration of society which is the special object of *Rerum Novarum* and *Quadragesimo Anno*. This particular reformation, as distinguished from that intended in other social encyclicals, is the reformation of the *social-economic* order.

It is for that reason that this encyclical should have appeal to those who have embraced socialism. For they were led to this choice, as Pope Pius points out by the excuse that, "The Church and those proclaiming attachment to the Church favor the rich, neglect the workers and have no concern for them."[28]

The whole teaching of *Rerum Novarum* and *Quadragesimo Anno* is here offered by the pope in denial of that allegation. And the basis of this teaching which should move the deserters is social justice.

NOTES FOR CHAPTER TWO

1. A review of the various classifications of social justice can be found in several studies of the subject, e.g.: J. Kleinhappl, "Der Begriff der Justitia Socialis und das Rundschreiben Quadragesimo Anno," *Zeitschrift für Katholische Theologie*, 1934, p. 364; Leo W. Shields, *The History and Meaning of Social Justice* (Notre Dame, 1941); William Ferree, *The Act of Social Justice* (Marianist Publications, Dayton, Ohio, 1951); V. Vangheluwe, "De Justitia Sociali," *Collationes Brugenses*, Vol. 43, 1947, pp.

309-321; 383-398; 436-448. A very brief summary is given by Vangheluwe, *Collationes Brugenses,* Vol. 44, 1948, pp. 306-309.

2. Ferree, *op. cit.,* p. 95.
3. *Quad. Anno,* n. 126.
4. *Ibid.,* n. 15.
5. *Rerum Novarum,* n. 3.
6. *Ibid.,* n. 6.
7. *Ibid.,* n. 4.
8. *Quad. Anno,* n. 2.
9. *Ibid.,* n. 3.
10. *Ibid.,* n. 4.
11. *Ibid.,* n. 7.
12. *Ibid.,* n. 54.
13. *Ibid.,* n. 57 and n. 58.
14. Messner, *op. cit.,* p. 124.
15. *Quad. Anno,* n. 71 and n. 74.
16. *Rerum Novarum,* n. 63.
17. *Casti Connubii,* p. 60.
18. *Quad. Anno,* n. 110.
19. *Ibid.,* n. 71.
20. *Ibid.,* n. 74.
21. *Ibid.,* n. 77.
22. *Ibid.,* n. 127 ff.
23. *Ibid.,* n. 18.
24. *Ibid.,* n. 100 and n. 101.
25. *Ibid.,* n. 110.
26. *Divini Redemptoris,* n. 51 and n. 52.
27. *Quad. Anno,* n. 126.
28. *Ibid.,* n. 124.

CHAPTER TWO
STUDY AIDS

Review Questions:

What are some of the various opinions about the nature of social justice?

What is the place of social justice in the teaching of *Quadragesimo Anno?*

From a study of *Quadragesimo Anno* what grounds are there for saying that social justice is a form of justice restricted to the economic order?

What is the relationship between the encyclicals *Quadragesimo Anno* and *Rerum Novarum?*

What was the particular social problem which concerned Leo XIII in the writing of *Rerum Novarum?*

What is meant by "the social question"?

Is social justice concerned with the common good?

Does the concern of social justice with the common good immediately identify social justice and legal justice?

What is the common good of the economic order?

Does social justice affect and oblige men precisely because they are "citizens" of a State?

What is the demand of social justice with regard to the distribution of wealth?

With regard to wages, does social justice immediately regulate the individual wage contract?

What does social justice command with regard to the wage system?

Is social justice a synonym for economic justice?

How is social justice contrasted with free competition as a principle of economic life?

Do the encyclicals condemn the system of capitalism in itself?

What are the abuses of capitalism that are condemned?

What, in summary, are the areas of social life to which the remedy of social justice must be applied according to *Quadragesimo Anno*?

In the encyclical, *Divini Redemptoris:*

Who are indicated as the subjects of the obligations of social justice?

What is to be the result of the realization of social justice?

What violations of social justice are scored?

Discussion Topics:

The effect of the distribution of wealth on economic prosperity.

Satisfaction of human wants as the purpose of economic activity.

Reflection of moral principles in economic practices and institutions.

Determination of the value of human labor.

Suggested Readings:

Bakke and Kerr, *Unions, Management and the Public* (New York: Harcourt, Brace, 1948), pp. 702–758.

Cahill, E., S.J., *The Framework of a Christian State* (Dublin: M. H. Gill and Son, 1932), Chap. XIV.

Due, John F., *Intermediate Economic Analysis* (Chicago: R. D. Irwin, Inc., 1950), pp. 350–379.

Hansen, A. H., *Business Cycles and National Income* (New York: Norton and Co., 1951), pp. 557–578.

Harriss, C. Lowell, *The American Economy* (Chicago: R. D. Irwin, Inc., 1953), pp. 702–722.

Messner, J., *Social Ethics*, pp. 129–132, 249–280, 697–715.

Mulcahy, R., S.J., *The Economics of Heinrich Pesch*, Chap. 2.

Nell-Breuning, O., S.J., *Reorganization of Social Economy*, pp. 171–191.

Shister, Joseph, *Economics of the Labor Market* (New York: Lippincott, 1949), pp. 543–555.

Social Justice and Ownership

RESTRICTED SPHERE OF SOCIAL JUSTICE

SOCIAL obligations go far beyond the economic sphere, and the common good of society toward which they are directed comprehends and complements every phase of temporal life. But they are not all the objects of social justice in its precise and technical sense despite the name that justice bears. From the positive sources of the encyclicals, from which principally the true meaning of social justice in Catholic social teaching is to be gathered, there is no positive warrant for extending the virtue to all the rights and duties implied in legal (and distributive) justice. On the other hand, social justice is always used by the encyclicals in connection with the economic order, with the common economic good, a restriction which cannot be predicated of traditional legal justice.

This initial restriction of social justice on the evidence of the encyclicals gives a fruitful lead to an understanding of its nature. Following that lead we can more easily determine those elements by which the various virtues are defined and distinguished one from another, as those elements affect social justice. Virtues and species of virtues are diversified, according to St. Thomas, by their relationship to different ends;[1] by the matter with which they are concerned and the particular aspect under which it concerns them — by their objects, that is, both "material" and "formal";[2] and, in the case of justice, by the persons who are the subjects of the rights and subjects of the obligations which justice regulates.[3] All these, as they refer to social justice, must be considered to arrive at some understanding of its nature.

THE END OF SOCIAL JUSTICE

The end of social justice (as has been indicated in the preceding section) is the common economic good, the common good of that area of human activity which looks to the adaptation of useful material goods to the attainment of the temporal prosperity of the human person. The nature of this common good follows from all that has been previously said of the dignity of human personality and of the subordination of material goods to the use of man as a person.

That material goods should serve the use of the human person is their prime destination in the plan of God. That they should serve the use of *all* men follows from the fact that all men are equal in their possession of personality, for the development of which material goods are destined by the Creator. Universal access to a human sufficiency of material goods is required of properly ordered economic activity which looks to the management of those goods. And the common good of the economic order consists in such a condition of economic organization and affairs that to each and every human person are offered all those material goods which are sufficient to supply the necessities of *human* life and which are the fundamental requisites of the temporal happiness of the human person.

In a simple, primitive order (we can imagine a family living a sort of Robinson Crusoe existence) this purpose of economic activity is clear and reasonable. The members work building a dwelling, raising produce, making clothes — all to supply the needs of the whole family, to satisfy legitimate human desires. To produce for the sake of the goods produced would, in these circumstances, seem absurd. To refuse to share the results would be suicide.

Yet with the advance of civilization, with the complication of economic activity, especially in a "money" economy like our own, this clarity of vision disappears. Competition replaces co-operation. Individual profit becomes the goal instead of common prosperity. Goods, money, have come to be sought for their own sake.

> In the human judgments which mould the economic system values have in fact been reversed. — Instead of being considered as a mere feeder enabling the living organism, which the productive undertaking is, to produce the necessary material, equipment and replenishment, money has become to be considered *the living organism.* — Values have been revised, and the immediate consequence is — to establish the whole economy under the supreme regulation of the laws and the fluidity of the *sign* money, predominating over the *thing,* commodities useful to mankind.[4]

The cause of this perversion is materialism and the neglect of the dignity of the human person. The occasion is the complexity of modern economic life with its resultant lack of personal relationships and reduction of accountability, which offers to selfish materialism the opportunity it needs to come to maturity and produce its natural progeny: "want in the midst of plenty."

New elements appear, or rather, elements which were present in the primitive economic order but taken for granted in its simplicity assume a new importance as the economic order grows: the elements of distribution or exchange and of the division of labor.

Distribution does not present the difficulties in the case of the imagined self-contained family living immediately on the land that it does in the complex life of crowded cities. The farmer and his family are the consumers as well as the producers of their material supplies. The members of the family are closely bound together. The necessity of the co-operation of each, and the part that each contributes to the common stock is clearly seen. The result of the labor of each is a complete product destined to supply the various known wants of all. There is no necessity of any medium of exchange to effect the distribution of the products of their different tasks.

But in our highly developed economic system all is different. Exchange plays such an important part in modern economic life and has so thoroughly transformed it that it can be characterized by the name of "economy of exchange."

Division of labor, too, becomes highly specialized in contrast with the primitive order. The immense market that densely populated cities offer makes it possible for a farmer to concentrate all his efforts on a single crop, wheat, for example; for a baker to bake only bread from the wheat; for a manufacturer to specialize in the production of baker's ovens; and for an individual to earn his living screwing ovens together.

These two factors effect a complete transformation of economic life. The close unity that held between the members of the simple economic order is gone, and the importance of the contribution of each to the common effect is not so apparent. Hardly any article is produced for the use of the one producing it. The man who stands at one end of a moving belt may scarcely know the man who stands at the other, though both are working on the same product. The result of the work of each is often not a complete product at all, but only a part to be passed on to others for completion. And the ultimate user of the finished product is unknown to the man who starts the work of production. For between them stands a group of middlemen who sell the products for money which buyers have received in the form of wages in exchange for their services in the whole productive process.

Add to these considerations the fact that the tools and machines with which men work are usually the property of still another man or of an impersonal, intangible "corporation," and the complexity of the situation is increased.

Yet the purpose of production, as the purpose of the goods produced, must remain the same in the more advanced economic organization as it was in the primitive example considered. That is the thematic proposition of *Quadragesimo Anno* (n. 75), repeated in *Divini Redemptoris* (n. 52):

> For then only will the social economy be rightly established and attain its purposes when all and each are supplied with all the goods that the wealth and resources of nature, technical achievement and the social organization of economic life can furnish. And these goods ought indeed to be enough both to meet the demands of necessity and decent comfort and to advance people to that happier and fuller condition of life which, when it is wisely cared for, is not only no hindrance to virtue but helps it greatly.

THE OBJECT OF SOCIAL JUSTICE

To obtain this condition of affairs whereby all will have access to such material goods is the purpose of social justice. Material goods, then, wealth, or the product of economic activity, goods apt to satisfy the rational needs and desires of men, are the things with which it is particularly concerned. And social justice concerns itself with these goods in terms of their destination for the use of all men.

In the terminology of scholastic philosophy it would be said that the material object of social justice is wealth; its formal object, the ordination of this wealth to the service of all men. The requirement of social justice is that wealth be so administered as to safeguard the good of all, to serve the needs of all. The *justum*, which, in the analysis of St.

Thomas, is the object of justice, becomes, in relation to social justice, the material goods of the world in so far as they are intended for the use of all men.

From this consideration emerges the cardinal fact of a special relationship between social justice and the institution of private property. For material goods which are to serve the use of all are, for the most part, the object of private possession. Some, it is true, are publicly owned; but, by and large, the things which affect the daily life of men most commonly are privately owned. The things by which man lives, feeds himself, is clothed, sheltered, transported, the instruments by which all these are produced and fashioned, the means by which they are exchanged are owned by individuals or private groups.

This special concern of social justice with the institution of private property receives further confirmation from reflection on the formal object of social justice: the ordination of material goods to the use of all men.

Enunciated by way of principle, that formal object becomes the metaphysical basis of the natural law doctrine of private property itself: Material goods exist for the use of all men as persons, to serve the human needs of all in a manner becoming the rational nature of man.

The importance of this principle must be underlined. Neglect of it as the basis of private ownership has led to much misunderstanding, misinterpretation, and maligning of the Church's teaching in the matter. And this has been due in some cases even to the presentation of that teaching in Catholic textbooks. So intent are these on establishing the right of private ownership and defending it against communism or socialism that the social aspect of property, which flows from the principle and on which the whole program of social justice of the encyclical pivots, appears almost as an afterthought which the abuses of property make necessary.

SOCIAL ASPECT OF OWNERSHIP

Examination of the encyclicals and of St. Thomas shows this social aspect of ownership to be no pragmatic appendage but an integral and essential part of the complete doctrine. It is expressly contained in the arguments which establish the right. Thus, Pius XI writes in *Quadragesimo Anno*:[5] "Nature, rather the creator Himself has given man the right of ownership not only that individuals may be able to provide for themselves and their families but also that the goods which the Creator has destined for the entire family of mankind may through this institution truly serve this purpose." And, again,[6] "The division of goods which results from private ownership was established by nature itself in order that created things may serve the needs of mankind in fixed and stable order."

It is the same principle which dictates the articles on private property found in the *Summa* of St. Thomas. Material goods exist for the use of men as rational creatures made in the image of God.[7] They are for the use of all men therefore, for in all men this image is found.

For this purpose private possession is necessary. But in view of this same purpose St. Thomas makes a distinction between the right of private property itself *(potestas procurandi et dispensandi)* and the "use" of property.[8] The former is required for three reasons. First, a solicitous administration of material goods would be impossible without it: Men ordinarily need the stimulus of personal ownership. Second, it is needed to avoid confusion and bring order to human affairs. And, last, the peace of human society depends on the contentment it brings. None of these could be had without private ownership, which is not only licit but "necessary for human life." As far as the "use" of property is concerned, however, men should consider their goods as "common" — ready for the service of all who need them.

In the whole argument of St. Thomas, as in that of the encyclicals, it is the purpose of material goods that justifies and controls the institution of private property. Property, then, is not a thing prescribed for its own sake and absolutely by the natural law. What is prescribed is that men — all men — should use material goods for the proper sustentation of human, personal, and family life. Private property is but the means that goods may serve this purpose in a manner in keeping with the dignity of human nature. It is necessary, not in itself, but because of the consequences, because without it material goods ordinarily could not attain their end in an orderly and peaceful way.

Division of property thus is legitimate and commanded in so far as it is necessary for the safeguarding of the ideal end of material goods. And this destiny is also the formal object of social justice.

SUBJECTS OF RIGHTS AND DUTIES

Granted the validity of the preceding analysis with regard to the object and purpose of social justice, the subjects of the rights and the subjects of the duties of that virtue can now more easily be determined.

The subjects of the rights of social justice are all men for the service of whom, as persons, the goods of this world are made. The subjects of its obligations, on the other hand, are those on whom the administration of property depends.

Primarily, as is evident, the duties of social justice will fall on the actual owners of property. Each and every person or group, possessing the goods which God has destined for the use of all, becomes responsible under God for the attainment of that destiny. Their obligations will differ in degree and kind as their amounts and types of property differ (a question which will be taken up in subsequent sections), but they rest on men as owners of property.

Others, too, besides actual owners can be bound by duties of social justice, according to *Quadragesimo Anno*. The "non-owning working class" can violate the law of social justice as well as the "class of the wealthy." But this violation also consists in the frustration of the purpose of property and material goods. By the pressures they can bring to bear, by their demands, by agitation, nonowners can affect the disposition and distribution of property in such a way as to defeat its natural purpose.

Quadragesimo Anno indicates two such instances. The nonowning violate social justice, the encyclical tells us,[9] when they would exclude any title to ownership except that of labor, impeding by that claim the distribution of the benefits of economic progress among the variety of contributors required for that very progress. And, again, in a later section[10] where the encyclical speaks of wages, "nonowning" workers are certainly included among those who violate social justice by attempting to regulate the wage rate without consideration of its effect on the volume of employment and, consequently, on the common good.

OWNERSHIP THE CENTRAL THEME

Further confirmation of the concern of social justice with the institution of ownership is found in an analysis of the doctrinal section of *Quadragesimo Anno*. This is the second main division of the encyclical, contained in numbers forty-one to ninety-nine. The purpose of this part of *Quadragesimo Anno* is to defend, explain, and develop more fully the principles, previously proposed by Pope Leo XIII, governing the solution of the socioeconomic question. From an examination of this section it is clear that the reform to be effected by social justice is built around the institution of ownership.

Here, after a preliminary defense of the Church's authority

to speak on social and economic matters (nn. 41–44), five logically connected subjects are discussed. First is the subject of ownership itself.

The right of property is put down as the juridical fundament of a sound economic order. Against the tenets of socialism, *Quadragesimo Anno* recalls by allusion what Leo XIII had said[11] about the institution of ownership: "Let it be regarded, therefore, as established that in seeking help for the masses this principle before all is to be considered as basic, namely, that private ownership must be preserved inviolate."

The teaching of Pius XI is then devoted to an exposition of the double character — individual and social — of property and to an emphasizing of the duties inherent in ownership (nn. 44–52).

The next section (nn. 53–58) treats of the members of the economic order, Capital and Labor, from the point of view of their mutual relationship in the matter of ownership and distribution of wealth. The titles of ownership and the division of property have been a source of bitter conflict between the two parties. Capital claimed all for itself, according to the iron economic laws of the liberals, Labor, espoused by the socialists and "intellectuals," has gone to the opposite extreme, laying claim to the "whole product." Both have been wrong, forgetting that "however the earth may be apportioned among private owners, it does not cease to serve the common interests of all." But the fact is undeniable that the distribution of property and wealth has been defeating the end which God intends — that it "is laboring today under the gravest evils due to the huge disparity between the few exceedingly rich and the unnumbered propertyless." The remedy is a distribution according to the norms of social justice.

The goal sought by *Rerum Novarum* and *Quadragesimo*

Anno is the subject matter of the next section (nn. 59–62): the redemption of the nonowning workers — the redemption of the proletariate. The "huge disparity," mentioned above, must be corrected by an equitable distribution of the fruits of production enabling the workers to increase their property and escape their proletarian status of insecurity.

Logically the following paragraphs (63–75) take up the question of the means to this goal — the question of wages and salaries by which alone "the nonowning workers, by industry and thrift, advance to the state of possessing some little property."

And, finally, the fifth division of this doctrinal part of the encyclical (nn. 76–99) is devoted to a consideration of the *conditio sine qua non* of the realization of the papal program: the restoration of social order by reformation of institutions. Here is the heart of the encyclical in what has become known as the "Papal Plan," the plan of the vocational organization of society. But still the concern of the encyclical is the institution of property and its proper ordination. "What we have thus far stated regarding an equitable distribution of property and regarding just wages concerns individual persons and only indirectly touches social order" are the words that introduce this discussion. To make possible the distribution needed for the common good, social reorganization according to an organic concept of society is required, doing away with the conflict of classes.

Thus, ownership — its defense, its purpose, its nature, its spread — becomes the unifying concept of these principal doctrinal points of the encyclical. A common theme runs through each point developed, the same theme which was later expressed by Pope Pius XII in his encyclical *Sertum Laetitiae:* "The fundamental point of the social question is this, that the goods created by God for all men should in the same way reach all."[12]

And since private ownership is the institution by which this shall be accomplished that proposition may be rephrased: "The fundamental point of the social question is this, that the institution of property be guided and directed to its proper end." That guidance and direction is the special purpose of social justice. True, it is the effect of many virtues; it supposes, as the encyclical stresses, a return to the principles of the gospel. Yet, as has been indicated, it calls especially for the practice of social justice. The particular reform of this encyclical is specifically based on the virtue of social justice.

SOCIAL JUSTICE AND LEGAL JUSTICE

In this concern of social justice with the institution of property ownership and with men as the owners and administrators of property is found another reason for asserting a difference between "social" justice and "legal" justice. Legal justice regulates the citizen-state relationship; social justice does not.[13]

Social justice may indeed affect the state and may be involved in the civil order; and this can happen in two ways. First, the state itself may be bound immediately by duties of social justice. In such a case, however, the state is subject to these duties not precisely because it is a state, but because, as a moral person, it is the owner of property which though in this case "public," still shares the purpose of all property: the service of all men. Second, the state, as a state, will have the duty and also the right of exacting and making possible the fulfillment of social justice on the part of the members of society in view of the common good. But this duty and its corresponding right, in themselves, pertain to legal rather than to social justice.

The province of legal justice can be described in these words of Messner: "The rights and duties of legal justice rest on men in politically organized communities. The duties of that justice are the duties that the members, as parts, have to the whole; the rights are those of the whole to the cooperation of the members. Both are formulated in the laws of the land."[14] Social justice, in contrast, does not necessarily suppose membership in organized society. It imposes its duties in virtue of the ordination of the goods of the world to the use of all men. Whether men live in civil society or not, independently of the legal enactments of governors and legislatures, that ordination remains, effecting its bonds of mutual rights and duties. Social justice rests on men, not as citizens, but as owners and administrators of property.

Within the framework of a definite national economy, it is true, and according to the variations of that economy, the duties of owners will be defined and particularized. Ownership will carry different duties in prosperous and pauperized lands, in industrial and rural peoples, in times of boom and depression. The concrete realization of social justice, as the acts of any virtue, will vary according to the context of circumstances which effect closer bonds of charity or justice between men. The general obligation of using one's goods for the service of all men finds its immediate application in obligations toward those who are most closely related by family, vocational, or civil ties. And these duties, in so far as they touch upon a national economy, may become duties of legal justice exacted by law.

Yet, such prescriptions of law are merely the determinants of a duty already existing in an indeterminate manner: the duty of using property for the good of all — the duty imposed by social justice. Legal justice commands the acts of social justice as it does the acts of all other virtues. "To define these duties in detail" (duties of the right use of property) "when necessity requires and the natural law has not done so, is the function of those in charge of the state. Therefore, public authority under the guiding light always of the natural and divine law can determine more accurately upon consideration of the true requirements of the common good, what is permitted and what is not permitted to owners in the use of their property."[15]

THE INTERNATIONAL ORDER

A further indication that social justice is not the same as the traditional legal justice is found in the fact that whole peoples or nations can be the terms of social justice. It is not confined to the limits of an organized society but stretches as far as the purpose of the goods it governs: to all mankind. Thus one nation which in its natural resources would have a practical monopoly on a certain type of raw material would be bound in social justice to allow other peoples a reasonable access to those goods.

This point is not passed over without notice by *Quadragesimo Anno*. In the midst of the discussion of the restoration of social justice as the directing principle of economic life (nn. 88–91), there is a brief broadening of vision from the national to the international economy: "Furthermore, since the various nations largely depend on one another in economic matters and need one another's help, they should strive with a united purpose and effort to promote by wisely conceived pacts and institutions a prosperous and happy international cooperation in economic life."[16]

A very noticeable obscurity appears at this point in the explanation of some of the proponents of the theory that "social" and "legal" justice are one and the same.

The theories considered here acknowledge the extension of social justice to the international sphere. They admit that the universal human society is a subject of rights in social justice.[17] Yet, the difficulty may be legitimately raised as to whether the "legal" justice of St. Thomas obtains in this universal society. The universal society of mankind is not yet a perfect society, nor a political society. It is only incipiently or inchoatively such. How the "legal" justice of St. Thomas, which, according to his teaching,[18] is in the ruler principally and "architectonically" and in the subjects secondarily and "ministratively," is strictly applicable to this society is not entirely clear. "Rulers" and "subject" are not to be found in an unorganized society.

Perhaps this is a too literal insistence on the words of the text of St. Thomas. Certainly there are authors of no slight authority who affirm duties of "general" justice in the natural international society as it now exists.[19] But the fact remains that the attempt to identify social justice with legal justice in this international field does involve further obscurities.

Thus, Vangheluwe makes the state, as a perfect society, the subject of the rights of social justice, because it "is the subject *in which resides the right* to demand of its citizens those acts which are necessary for the common good; in other words, society itself is the *subject to which* the duties of social justice are owed."[20]

The author, however, does not restrict this "subject" to the national state; the "universal society of mankind" is also possessed of rights of social justice. This universal society, on the other hand, does not yet exist as an organized body with its own power of jurisdiction. And, therefore, the duties of social justice owed to it are not demanded by "laws" (*usu jurisdictionis*) of the universal society. These duties are fulfilled by the fact that the rulers of the different nations obtain the common good of the members of their particular civil societies in such a way that at the same time the good of all humanity is promoted.[21]

The subjects of the duties of international social justice are, according to this theory, "each and every member of the natural society of mankind, who must provide for the universal common good either by himself, in so far as he is able, or, most of all, through the instrumentality of the rulers of his own civil society."[22]

From this it would seem to follow that the universal society is the subject of rights of social justice only in an indirect way.

Critics of Vangheluwe's theory, who, nevertheless, defend with him the identification of social and legal justice, affirm that the universal society "despite the mere futurity of its appropriate organization" is the *"only immediate qualifier"* as the subject of rights in social justice.[23] The state is a *mediate* (through the medium of the demands of universal society) subject of those rights. The subjects of the duties of social justice are all individuals who are "obligated immediately to human society in its care for the universal common good, and mediately to the particular society necessarily engaged in caring for some part of the universal common good."[24]

Both of these theories plunge the whole question of the obligations of social justice into the deeper obscurity of the future appropriate organization of international society, and involve the debatable question of the relative perfection of national states. Such involvement belies the clear discernibility of the duties of social justice which the papal encyclicals imply.

Nor is clarity added to the issue by stating that in social justice there is a "de-emphasis of the citizen-state relationship" and a "support of the nonpolitical individual-society relationship."[25] At least, clarity is not added if this statement be understood as explaining the identification of social justice with St. Thomas' legal justice. It does clarify, on the other hand, if it be understood as descriptive of the social duties of ownership.[26]

DEFINITION OF SOCIAL JUSTICE

At this point it is possible to formulate a definition of social justice in the light of the preceding analysis of the encyclicals' treatment of the virtue. That analysis led to several conclusions:

1. Social justice has as its peculiar province the socio-economic order, and has as its purpose the common economic good.

2. It is concerned, therefore, with the institution of property ownership which is directed to this same end.

3. More precisely, its formal object is the social aspect of property.

4. With respect to the other types of justice: social justice seems certainly to be distinct from commutative justice (a distinction which will hardly be denied in view of the statement of *Divini Redemptoris* that "besides commutative justice there is also social justice with its own set obligations"); and the distinction between social justice and legal (and/or distributive) justice is solidly founded.

Social justice can, therefore, be defined as: *a special species of justice, distinct from commutative, legal and distributive, which requires that material goods, even privately owned, shall serve the common use of all men.*[27]

NOTES FOR CHAPTER THREE

1. *Summa Theol.,* II–II, q. 47, a. 11.
2. *Ibid.,* a. 5; also I–II, q. 54, a. 2; II–II, q. 101, a. 3.
3. *Ibid.,* II–II, q. 58, a. 7 and a. 8.
4. Maritain, "Religion and Culture," in *Essays in Order,* ed. C. Dawson (New York: Sheed and Ward, 1940), p. 57.
5. N. 45.
6. N. 56.
7. *Summa Theol.,* II–II, q. 66, a. 1.
8. *Ibid.,* a. 2.
9. *Quad. Anno,* n. 57.

10. *Ibid.*, n. 74.

11. *Rerum Novarum,* n. 23.

12. Encyclical of Pius XII, Nov. 1, 1939 (*Catholic Mind,* Nov. 22, 1939), n. 50.

13. Similarly, social justice is distinguished from distributive justice which is "that form of justice which directs the community to share out burdens and benefits among its members in accordance with the proportionate equality implicit in the common good. Whereas legal justice directs the authority and the members to serve the common good, distributive justice operates contrariwise, directing the governing power to the good of the individual and group members" (Messner, *op. cit.,* p. 218). However, since the weight of adverse opinion favors the identification of social and legal justice, that is the distinction which needs explanation.

14. *Social Ethics,* p. 216.

15. *Quad. Anno,* n. 49.

16. *Ibid.*, n. 89.

17. V. Vangheluwe, *op. cit.,* p. 314; also, J. Schuyler, S.J., and J. Carmody, S.J., "Thoughts on Social Justice," *Social Order,* June, 1949, p. 248.

18. *Summa Theol.,* II–II, q. 58, a. 6.

19. A. Vermeersch, *Quaestiones de Justitia,* n. 54; and, J. LeClercq, *Lecons de Droit Naturel,* Vol. I, Chap. 4, n. 38.

20. Vangheluwe, *op. cit.,* p. 314.

21. *Ibid.*, p. 315.

22. *Ibid.*, p. 390.

23. Schuyler and Carmody, *op. cit.,* p. 248.

24. *Ibid.*, p. 253.

25. *Ibid.*

26. Both theories, too, might be criticized on the ground that, by implication at least, they would seem to deny a common teaching of Catholic scholars as to the nature of organized international society. The international society does not become a "state" whose members are the individual members of mankind. The members of organized international society are themselves "states" which retain in that organization their own relative autonomy and perfection. Cf. *Code of International Ethics* (Oxford: The Catholic Social Guild, 1946), pp. 11–12; Pius XII, 1944 Christmas Message; W. L. Lucey, *The International Society: Nature and Organization* (Worcester, College of the Holy Cross, 1948), pp. 17–18.

27. This definition is substantially the same as that at which Donat arrives: "Social justice, therefore, appears to be a special species of justice. Material goods, in as far as they, even though privately owned, are primarily destined to serve the use of all, are its formal object. It rests formally not on society as such, but upon all individuals. . . ." (*Ethica Specialis,* n. 72.) The method of deriving the definition, however, differs. The present study adds the support of the analysis of *Quadragesimo Anno* to Donat's conclusion. The elements of this definition are also found in Messner's *Social Ethics,* although a concise definition is not given there. Messner indicates: a distinction between legal and social justice (pp. 219–220); a restriction of social justice to the social-economic order (pp. 216, 700); a special concern of social justice with private ownership (pp. 792, 810).

CHAPTER THREE

STUDY AIDS

Review Questions:

Is there reason, on the evidence of the encyclicals, for saying that all social obligations are not the object of social justice in its precise meaning?

How are the different virtues distinguished from each other according to St. Thomas?

What is meant by the "material" and "formal" objects of a virtue?

What is the "end" of social justice?

How is the purpose of economic activity derived from a consideration of the dignity of man and the purpose of material goods?

What is the cause, and what is the occasion of the deviation of economic activity from its proper end?

What is the "material object" of social justice? What is its "formal object"?

How do these objects indicate a special concern of social justice with the institution of private property?

How is this special concern confirmed by consideration of the relationship between the basic principle of the natural law doctrine of private ownership and the formal object of social justice?

What is the fundamental principle of the natural law doctrine of private ownership?

What distinction does St. Thomas draw from this principle between the right of private property and the use of property?

Is the social aspect of property an essential part of the natural law doctrine of ownership?

Who are the subjects of the rights and duties of social justice?

Can "nonowners" as well as "owners" violate social justice?

What is the purpose of the doctrinal section of the encyclical, *Quadragesimo Anno* (nn. 41–99)?

What is the central theme of this section?

How is it developed?

How does the concern of social justice with the institution of property ownership indicate a difference between legal and social justice?

Who are the subjects of the duties and rights of legal justice?

Can social justice affect the State?

Does social justice suppose membership in an organized society?

How does such membership determine more concretely the duties of social justice?

Do the obligations of social justice extend to the international sphere?

In the light of the analysis of *Quadragesimo Anno,* what is the definition of social justice?

Discussion Topics:

The natural law basis of private ownership.

Individual and social aspects of private ownership.

Ownership and control in modern corporations.

National surpluses and aid to other nations.

Suggested Readings:

Gonella, Guido, *A World to Reconstruct,* trans. by T. L. Bous-caren, S.J. (Milwaukee: The Bruce Publishing Co., 1944), pp. 124–153.

Maritain, J., *Freedom in the Modern World* (New York: Scribner, 1936), Appendix I.

Michel, Virgil, O.S.B., "Ownership and the Human Person," *Review of Politics,* I (1939), pp. 155–177.

Messner, J., *Social Ethics,* pp. 785–800.

Nell-Breuning, O., S.J., *Reorganization of Social Economy,* pp. 94–122.

Ryan, Msgr. J. A., *Distributive Justice,* Chaps. I to VIII.

Sturzo, Luigi, *Inner Laws of Society* (New York: P. J. Kenedy and Sons, 1944), pp. 95–121.

Ward, Leo R., C.S.C., *Christian Ethics,* pp. 158–176.

Wright, John J., *National Patriotism in Papal Teaching* (Boston: Stratford Co., 1942), pp. 215–237.

Social Justice:
The Stewardship of Wealth

THE STEWARDSHIP OF WEALTH

THERE is nothing new in the virtue of social justice as just defined except the name. The social duties of wealth and property have always been an essential part of the Catholic tradition. No theologian who has taught under the guidance and authority of the Church has ever denied or questioned the social aspect of property, as Pope Pius XI points out.[1] The "Stewardship of wealth" is an idea that is constantly repeated in the writings of the Fathers of the Church, in St. Thomas, and in papal and episcopal documents which deal with the subject of ownership and its duties. "Social justice" is the modern term for this traditional "stewardship."

If this be so, several questions naturally arise. Very legitimately it is asked, "Why this change in name?" And, furthermore, "What in particular are these duties of stewardship? Are they any more than duties of charity?"

The answer to these questions presupposes the explanation of a double distinction, made by both *Rerum Novarum* and *Quadragesimo Anno* following the teaching of St. Thomas, with regard to property rights: the distinction between the right to possess and the right use of possessions; and the distinction (respecting the right use of property) between necessary and superfluous goods.

RIGHT OF OWNERSHIP AND USE

The first distinction is called by Leo XIII "the foundation" of the Church's teaching on the use of wealth: "On
the use of wealth, we have the excellent and extremely
weighty teaching, which, although found in a rudimentary
stage in pagan philosophy, the Church has handed down in
a completely developed form and causes to be observed not
only in theory but in everyday life. The *foundation of this
teaching* rests on this, that the just ownership of money is
distinct from the just use of money."[2]

In support of this statement the encyclical then quotes the
teaching of St. Thomas to which reference has previously
been made.

> It is lawful for man to own his own things. It is even neces-
> sary for human life. But if the question be asked: How ought
> a man to use his possessions? the Church replies without
> hesitation: "As to this point, man ought not regard external
> goods as his own, but as common so that, in fact, a person
> should readily share them when he sees others in need."[3]

Neglect of this distinction has been the cause of two errors,
both of which are scored by *Quadragesimo Anno* in its defense and explanation of the doctrine of Leo XIII on this
point. The first error is that of certain Catholic sociologists,
who in their zeal to rectify the social abuses of property went
so far as to brand every such abuse a violation of strict justice,
and who urged that the traditional definition of ownership
should be changed in such a way that it would expressly con-
tain the social duties of property. Pope Pius XI condemned
their exaggerations and ended the controversy they had
provoked.[4]

> In order to place definite limits on the controversies that
> have arisen over ownership and its inherent duties there must
> be first laid down as a foundation a principle established
> by Leo XIII: The right of property is distinct from its use.

That Justice called commutative commands sacred respect for the division of possessions and forbids invasion of others' rights through the exceeding of the limits of one's own property; but the duty of owners to use their property only in a right way does not come under this type of justice, but under other virtues, obligations of which "cannot be enforced by legal action." Therefore they are in error who assert that ownership and its right use are limited by the same boundaries.[5]

Hence, also, there is no need to change the definition of private property in order to express the social duties which are attached to the possession of wealth. It is not exact to say that property *is* a social function; rather, property *has* a social function. An owner is bound to make good use of his property but this is not an obligation of strict commutative justice; and that is why this obligation of social use should not be incorporated in the definition of the right which is founded on commutative justice and defined in terms of that justice.

At least, this group erred on the side of light. The other error, that of Liberalism, arising from the failure to distinguish between the right of ownership and its right use, went to the other bleak extreme. Identifying the juridical and moral boundaries of the right of property, or, rather, perhaps, excluding other moral considerations from the juridical institution, liberalism held that the only misuse of property consisted in the violation of rights of commutative justice. Practically this reduced abuses to theft, destruction of property, and the breaking of contracts.

This error no less than the first is condemned by the encyclical. Besides its individual aspect, property also has a social aspect looking to the common good, even though all the duties that arise therefrom "cannot be enforced by legal action." The distinction between right and use works two ways. Abuse of possessions does not always constitute a violation of commutative justice, in the terms of which the right of possession is defined; but neither does the right to possess leave the owner entirely free to use his property in any way.

> A man's superfluous income, that is, income which he does not need to sustain life fittingly and with dignity, is not left wholly to his own free determination. Rather the Sacred Scriptures and the Fathers of the Church constantly declare in the most explicit language that the rich are bound by a very grave precept to practice almsgiving, beneficence and munificence.[6]

NECESSARY AND SUPERFLUOUS GOODS

Here is introduced the second distinction, mentioned above, which is used by the encyclicals and St. Thomas in determining the social duties attached to ownership: the distinction between necessary and superfluous goods. It is with the latter especially (but not exclusively) that the duties of stewardship are connected. Goods needed for a decent human life, for support of family, for maintaining one's station in life becomingly and decently are known as "necessary" goods. They may be used exclusively for the individual and family advantage of the owners.[7] This is but a particularization and application of the common destination of material goods to attain which the institution of ownership is necessary. Goods possessed over and above these are called "superfluous." Such are to be used for the common good of all. If the right to superfluous goods meant the right to apply these goods exclusively to the advantage of the owner, then the prime destination of material goods would be frustrated and the foundation of private ownership would be destroyed.

In the matter, then, of superfluous goods, the right of the owner is a strict right of commutative justice. But, following the doctrine enunciated above, it is a right of administration for the common good, which is also a strict duty — the duty of stewardship.

Pope Leo XIII summed up his teaching on this point as follows:

> The substance of all this is the following: whoever has received from the bounty of God a greater share of goods, whether corporeal and external, or of the soul, has received them for this purpose, namely that he employ them for his own perfection and likewise, as a servant of Divine Providence, for the benefit of others.[8]

But are these duties of stewardship anything different from or more than duties of charity? The question is suggested by the fact that, generally speaking, textbooks in moral theology and philosophy append two natural limitations to the use of property which arise from the obligation of using one's property for the benefit of others. Those limitations are: the grave obligation of aiding another in the case of that other's "extreme" need — of aiding another, that is, whose life is endangered by want; and a general, vaguer obligation to help the ordinarily poor.

Both these limitations, in so far as they are obligations of positively using one's goods for the welfare of others, are put down as obligations of charity, not of justice of any kind. Justice may enter the picture in the case of extreme necessity, but in a negative way. It is admitted that a person in extreme need, other means failing, may take what he needs from the goods of another, provided this other is not reduced to a similar extreme want by the act. Such appropriation is a strict right; and, therefore, an owner who would positively prevent this act would be violating justice.[9] But this does not imply a duty of justice on the part of the owner of spontaneously giving that necessary aid.[10] Vermeersch even notes[11] that there is no violation of justice on the part of one who conceals from a person in extreme need, even with a lie, the fact that he possesses property.

The obligations of stewardship that naturally limit the use of ownership seem thus to be restricted to duties of charity. By what right, then, can these duties of stewardship be called duties of "social justice"?

SOCIAL JUSTICE AND CHARITY

A preliminary answer to this question is given in the words of Fr. Donat:

> That these (social duties of wealth) are duties of charity is clear. But the natural and Christian feeling has always been, at least obscurely, that many of them are more than debts of charity and that their violation contains an injury. . . . In recent times, in which the grave evils in the division of temporal goods has greatly sharpened this feeling, the opinion has become quite common that there is question of true justice. And rightly. For justice is the virtue giving each his own. It looks, therefore, to a thing which is owed to another as his and which is ordered to his good. . . . Now material goods are ordained to the use of all, and therefore everyone can claim them as his own, even those which have become the property of others, not in the sense that they may claim determinately this or that good from this or that particular person, but indeterminately in the sense that they, too, should have a sufficiency for living from material goods. And therefore insofar as this is denied them, they are deprived of something owed to them and justice is violated.[12]

The author then goes on to say that this justice has been given the name of social justice by *Quadragesimo Anno*.

Turning again to that encyclical, it does seem that its teaching forces us to urge the duties of social use of wealth, in present-day circumstances, as more than duties of charity. That some kind of justice is involved seems evident from the fact that the neglect of these duties has been the cause of the violation of a strict right.

Condemning the false principles of liberalism, Pope Pius XI writes:

> Property, that is, "Capital," has undoubtedly long been able to appropriate too much to itself. Whatever was produced, whatever returns accrued, capital claimed for itself, hardly leaving to the worker enough to restore and renew his strength. For the doctrine was preached that all accumulation of capital falls by an absolutely insuperable economic law to the rich, and that by the same law the workers are given over and bound to perpetual want, to the scantiest of livelihoods. . . . These false ideas . . . have been vigorously assailed and not by those alone who through them were being *deprived of their innate right* to obtain better conditions.[13]

The "innate right" here spoken of is the right which Catholic philosophy holds to be the congenital right of every human person: the right to acquire private property to that extent which is necessary for individual and family life in conformity with the dignity of human personality. The affirmation of this universal strict right to acquire property, and the affirmation that the actuation of that right on the part of so many is impossible because of the management of property, argues to more than a violation of charity in the use of wealth.

Again, in the words of *Quadragesimo Anno:* " . . . the immense multitude of the non-owning workers on the one hand and the enormous riches of certain very wealthy men on the other establish an unanswerable argument that the riches which are so abundantly produced in our age of 'industrialism,' as it is called, are not rightly distributed and equitably made available to the various classes of people."[14]

And the encyclical immediately goes on: "Therefore with all our strength . . . we must strive that at least in the future the abundant fruits of production will accrue equitably to those who are rich and will be distributed in ample sufficiency among the workers. . . ."[15]

Resuming the pertinent words of the citations: an accumulation of riches which causes the deprivation of an "innate right," a distribution of property which is neither "right" nor "equitable," the prescribed remedy — that ample sufficiency be supplied to the workingman by seeing to it that the future share of the rich is "equitable" — all seem to indicate that the violation of the social duties of property, which the encyclical condemns, is a violation not only of charity but also of some kind of justice.

The use of the term "social justice" to describe the virtue to which these duties of the stewardship of wealth pertain is thus readily understandable. They imply more than duties of charity, yet are not duties of strict commutative justice. They pertain neither to legal nor distributive justice strictly because they do not affect men precisely as members of organized society, but rather as the administrators of property. Yet they do belong to the sphere of justice in so far as on their fulfillment depends the right of every man to provide for himself and his family. And that "justice" is "social" rather than individual because its duties are based not on the determinate claims of any definite individuals to particular goods but on the destination of material goods to the common good of all men as persons.

Because of this destination of material goods, the possessor of superfluous wealth has a duty of using these superfluities for the common good — for the good of those who need them. This is a duty of the stewardship of wealth which, according to our analysis of the encyclicals, the pope calls "social justice."

SOURCE OF THE RIGHT TO OWNERSHIP OF SUPERFLUOUS GOODS

As mentioned before, neglect of the fundamental principle on which the right of private ownership is based has been the cause of much misinterpretation of the Church's doctrine in the matter of property. Failure to interpret the right to superfluous goods in the light of that principle completely distorts that doctrine. For, on ultimate analysis, the justification of the right to possess such goods is reduced to this: that there may be a responsible, orderly management of material things for the use of all. The right to possess superfluous goods connotes essentially the duty of using such possessions for the good of others. Brief reflection on the argument establishing the right of private ownership confirms this contention.

Material goods are made for the use and service of man in a way becoming his dignity as a person. They are intended for the proper self-development of free intelligent persons destined by nature to lead a social life in family and state. "It is," reads *Divini Redemptoris* (n. 30), "according to the dictates of reason that all earthly things should be for the use and benefit of man, and so through him be referred to the Creator." They are not made for the use of this or that man, or for any number of selected men, but for all men as possessing human personality.

From this principle is immediately deduced the inalienable, inviolable right of use. Every man has the right from nature to use these material things, since they are the necessary means of preserving his life and working out his destiny.

The further question of the right of private ownership of these goods is then easily established. For, considering the nature of man (an intelligent, provident being, destined for family life, who, moreover, needs the stimulus of proprietorship for the care required in the management of material goods), that prime and congenital right of use could not be properly exercised without private ownership.

Such, in general outline, is the typical argument proving the right of private property. But this argument, on examination, does not *explicitly* prove the right of ownership which stands at the center of the social question today — the right to ownership of superfluous goods. Strictly and explicitly it proves the right to own what is *necessary* for the sustentation and development of life and the support of family. The human needs, absolute and conventional, of the individual evidently cannot be used to establish the right to goods which are superfluous to one's state, from the very admission that they are superfluous and not necessary.

Yet the right to such possession is a strict right. How is it derived? Only by a return to the fundamental principle of the purpose of material goods: their orderly service of all men as persons. Ownership is here necessary that there may be a responsible, intelligent, conscientious administration of material things to this end intended for them by God through the mediation of man.

The meaning and application of St. Thomas' "Common Use" is thus unmistakably clear. There rests on the owners of superfluous goods a strict obligation, arising from the fact of superfluity, to administer their goods so that the human needs of all individuals and classes in society be thereby satisfied — an obligation which flows directly from the very notions which justify ownership.

PRUDENCE IN STEWARDSHIP

Yet the disposition of superfluous goods for the service of all need not be a gratuitous distribution. The stewardship or management of property of this kind is a charge which must be carried out in an intelligent manner. It must look not only to present necessities but must also provide for the future needs of the community. It involves the use of prudence.

"It is not sufficient," as one writer on the subject points out,[16] "in view of the common good merely to relieve the present needs of the poor. Provision must be made for future needs, too, and for the right development of the whole social-economic life.

"For it is much better and more conducive to the common good if the number of the poor decreases by an increase in the number of those who can support themselves by their own labor. Hence it can happen that in some cases the common good requires that superfluous goods be used in founding or expanding various useful industries which will provide employment rather than in almsgiving, even though this may bring profit to the investor."

St. Thomas enunciates this doctrine in one pregnant sentence in the *Summa*.[17] After his very strong assertion that "Those things which some possess in superabundance are owed by natural right (*ex naturali jure debentur*) to the support of the poor," he added, "But, since there are many who are in need and it is impossible to help all with the same thing, the dispensation of one's own goods is committed to the choice of each, that by them he may come to the help of those who are in need."

This consideration sheds further light on the problem, already raised, of the relationship between "charity" and "social justice." It also points a way to a reconciliation between the restriction of duties of "stewardship" to duties of "charity," as it is found generally in the textbooks of moral theology, and the extension of these duties to a kind of "justice," as is indicated in the encyclicals.

Almsgiving and similar works of charity are one way of fulfilling the duties of stewardship. This no one will question. It is stated explicitly by *Quadragesimo Anno*:[18] "The rich are bound by a very grave precept to practice almsgiving." But the encyclical indicates that there are other ways of fulfilling these same duties. Among these other ways it mentions "the practice of munificence" (*magnificentiae*) and, more in detail, singles out "expending larger incomes so that opportunity for gainful work may be abundant" as an outstanding exemplification the virtue of munificence particularly suited to the needs of the times.[19]

Now munificence (*magnificentia*) according to the teaching of St. Thomas (whose work is here referred to by the encyclical), as distinguished from liberality, looks to the use of money not by way of *gift* but by way of expenses assumed in the accomplishment of some notable work. The duties of stewardship, therefore, are not merely duties of "giving away." Almsgiving and munificence are not synonyms. Neither are "almsgiving" and the duties of stewardship to be identified.

The "stewardship of wealth" is a universal expression that describes generically all those uses of wealth which safeguard the ideal purpose of material goods: the service of all men. But these uses, determined as they must be by the prudence of the "steward," will vary with varying concrete circumstances.

The method, therefore, of discharging the duties of stewardship may be one of several left to the choice of the possessor who should be guided in his choice by the needs of time and locality. The investment of money in a business organization is one such method. Almsgiving would be another. The loan of money or the leasing of property would be still another. The choice belongs to the owner of wealth; but the obligation is inescapable.

DEVELOPMENT OF DOCTRINE NECESSARY

It is true that traditional moral teaching, as found in the textbooks, while insisting on the distribution of superfluous goods and the care of the poor, seems mainly concerned with almsgiving and acts of charity as the means of distribution. An insistence today on a duty of social justice is not an indication of a change in principles but of a change in social economic conditions, to which the principles must be applied, which calls for a more complete exposition of the duties attending the possession of wealth.

The moral manuals, as a rule, treat directly the duty of relieving the private necessity of the neighbor which rests on the possessors of superfluous goods, and only indirectly the social character of property which imposes duties of social use and administration by the very fact of superfluity. This latter point is not entirely neglected. Yet, even where it is given consideration, its treatment seems to be secondary. Thus, Vermeersch notes briefly, at the end of his explanation of the duties of almsgiving[20] that, today, the wealthy, in the use of their property, should consider themselves "less as masters (owners) than as managers, as providentially appointed stewards, managing, for the utility of all, a heritage which, in its prime destination, is truly common to all." Even this "stewardship," however, is urged under the heading of charity.

This identification of the duties of stewardship with works of charity may be due to the fact that at the time when traditional doctrine was formulated, those who were able and willing to work could find a permanent place in the social-economic society of the time. The class that needed special care was the class of unfortunates unable to help themselves: the class of the "deserving poor," and that help was to be given to them by works of charity.

Hence, also, looking to individual cases, moralists restricted their consideration of stewardship to these acts of charity. The development of their doctrine was devoted to discussing and determining the gravity of this obligation of almsgiving. According to the degree of "need" to be relieved in each case they distinguished various grades of obligation. "Extreme" need or "grave" need that comes close to "ex-

treme" impose a grave obligation on those who possess superfluous goods: "grave" need imposes a grave obligation, leav-
ing the donor, however, the option of bestowing his goods
on some other good cause; "common" need does not impose
a grave obligation, nor any obligation for a determined case,
but, to quote an approved authority: "All admit there is at
least a light (*venialem*) obligation of giving alms *sometimes,*
if one has wealth superfluous to nature and state of life."[21]

Since the time of this formulation of doctrine, however,
and with the rise and growth of industrial capitalism, a
new economic class has come into being: a proletariate. It is
with this class that the encyclicals are mainly concerned. It
is to the redemption of the proletariate that the reforms of
the encyclical are principally directed.[22]

A NEW MODERN NEED

And with the rise of this class a new kind of "need" has
arisen calling for a new examination and formulation of the
duties of ownership. This new "need" is a *general, social,
grave* need,[23] which results from a peculiarly modern type of
widespread, individual, common necessity. It is a "need"
which receives scant notice in textbook treatises, and one
which is not answered by the obligations there indicated.

This social need is not the same as that which, because of
the existence of a multitude of the poor, has always been
a fact, even in nonindustrial society. The dictum, "The poor
you have always with you," is perennially true due to the
ever present causes of personal misfortune, natural calam-
ities, accident, and avarice. But poverty, even widespread
poverty, and proletarianism are not synonymous. *Quadragesimo Anno* distinguishes between pauperism and proletarianism.[24] And though a certain poverty can be predicated
of the members of the proletariate, yet it is their rootless
insecurity which accurately describes them.[25]

The proletariate is described by the encyclical as "the immense multitude" of the nonowning workers[26] characterized by "that insecure lot in life in whose uncertainties nonowning workers are cast."[27] By definition the proletariate is "the class of workers of humble state, living from day to day on a salary barely sufficient, without savings, without security for tomorrow, without protection against economic risks."

Thus, the proletariate is not composed of those who are in extreme need, nor yet in grave need. They are not absolutely without means or income; they are not actually starving. Perhaps, in the future, with sickness, accident, or age, they may fall into the case of extreme need; but today they are not included. At most, the "need" of the proletariate would be described as "common," if we consider the individual members.

But the precarious economic conditions of these "propertyless," their great number, the huge disparity between them and the "few exceedingly rich," the resultant class struggle[28] — all effect a situation which must be remedied if public order, peace, and the tranquillity of human society are to be effectively defended.[29] A grave social danger exists, a general grave necessity in the insecurity of the rootless proletariate.

NORMAL AND AUXILIARY METHODS OF STEWARDSHIP

This "need" is not met by fulfillment merely of the traditional duties of charity. It imposes further duties called by the encyclical duties of social justice. Almsgiving and works of charity will always be duties of the stewardship of wealth. "Even supposing," says *Quadragesimo Anno*,[30] "that everyone should finally receive all that is due to him, the widest field for charity will always remain open." But in the present world all are not receiving all that is due. And consequently, "the distribution of created goods, which, as every discerning person knows, is laboring today under the gravest evils due to the huge disparity between the few exceedingly rich and the unnumbered propertyless, must be effectively called back to and brought into conformity with the norms of the common good, that is social justice."[31]

In other words, works of charity are an *auxiliary* means by which material goods come to their appointed end and the duties of the stewardship of wealth are fulfilled. But the first and essential duty which rests on the possessors of superfluous wealth today is so to administer their wealth as to allow all to attain, by work and wages, access to that property[32] which means security and the elimination of those social evils which are the symptoms of liberalism in our modern economic regime — the existence of a proletariate and the existence of chronic, widespread unemployment. Right order and the plan of God demand that the *normal* way in which material goods attain their purpose is by such management of property and such social organization that every able and free man, every father of a family should be able to provide for himself and his family.

Men have a strict right to life — to human life; and when work is the only way they have of attaining the means of life, men have a strict right to work. It is a right which immediately imposes on those who have superfluous wealth, who possess the means of production, a duty of so administering their wealth that those who are able and willing may, by their own efforts, rise at least to that minimum of economic security which the dignity of human personality demands.

This is not merely a duty of charity. It is the restoration of society to that order wherein the strict right of every human person to a decent life is capable of fulfillment. It is a duty of social justice urged by the very arguments that legitimatize the right of property.

NOTES FOR CHAPTER FOUR

1. *Quad. Anno,* n. 45.
2. *Rerum Novarum,* n. 35.
3. *Ibid.,* n. 36.
4. With regard to this controversy, cf. V. Cathrein, S.J., "Uberfluss und Almosen," *Theologisch-praktische Quartalschrift,* 1929, p. 674; and A. Vermeersch, "Sociale Krise und Reformtheorien," *ibid.,* p. 687.
5. *Quad. Anno,* n. 47.
6. *Ibid.,* n. 50.
7. *Rerum Novarum,* n. 36.
8. *Ibid.*
9. G. F. Waffelaert, *De Justitia,* I, n. 35; II, n. 189, c.
10. Noldin, *Summa Theol. Moralis,* II, n. 424, e.
11. *Quaestiones de Justitia,* n. 239.
12. J. Donat, S.J., *Ethica Specialis,* 5th edition, 1934, n. 71.
13. *Quad. Anno,* n. 54.
14. *Ibid.,* n. 60.
15. *Ibid.,* n. 61.
16. C. Damen, C.Ss.R., "De Recto Usu Superfluorum," *Analecta Gregoriana,* Vol. IX, 1935, p. 78.
17. *Summa Theol.,* II–II, q. 66, a. 7.
18. N. 50.
19. N. 51.
20. Vermeersch, *Theol. Moralis,* II, n. 100.
21. *Ibid.,* II, n. 96, d.
22. *Quad. Anno,* n. 59.
23. *Ibid.,* n. 62.
24. *Ibid.,* n. 60.
25. Cf. Henri Godin and Yves Daniel, *France, Pays de Mission?* (Paris: Les Editions du Cerf, 1943), p. 22.
26. *Quad. Anno,* n. 60.
27. *Ibid.,* n. 61.
28. *Ibid.,* nn. 57 and 83.
29. *Ibid.,* n. 62.
30. *Ibid.,* n. 137.
31. *Ibid.,* n. 58.
32. *Ibid.,* n. 63.

CHAPTER FOUR

STUDY AIDS

Review Questions:

Is social justice a "new" virtue?

Under what name have the duties of social justice always been known in Catholic tradition?

What two distinctions with regard to property ownership are basic to an understanding of social justice?

Where are these distinctions found?

What errors follow from a failure to distinguish between the right of ownership itself and the right use of property?

Are all abuses of private property violations of commutative justice?

Should all the social obligations of ownership be expressed in the definition of the right of ownership?

Supposing the observance of commutative justice, is an owner then morally free to use his property any way he wishes?

What is "necessary," what "superfluous" income?

With regard to superfluous goods, may an owner apply these exclusively to his own advantage?

Is the obligation of sharing superfluous goods an obligation of strict commutative justice?

Is it certainly an obligation of charity?

Do the encyclicals indicate that there is some kind of justice involved in this obligation?

Why is the term "social justice" an apt term to describe this obligation?

Is the right to the ownership of superfluous goods a strict right?

Is the right to the ownership of "necessary" goods proved in exactly the same way as the right to "superfluous" goods?

What is meant by saying that the stewardship of wealth involves the use of prudence?

Are almsgiving and works of charity the only ways in which an owner can fulfill his duties of stewardship?

What are some other ways?

What reason is there for the insistence in traditional moral teaching on the duties of almsgiving?

What reason is there for an insistence on other duties in modern circumstances?

What new "need," determining the duties of stewardship, has arisen with the rise of industrialism?

Is *Quadragesimo Anno* especially concerned with this "need"?

What is meant by the "proletariate"?

Is there a difference between proletarianism and pauperism?

Do the traditional obligations of almsgiving adequately meet modern social-economic needs?

What is the normal means for the fulfillment of the duties of the stewardship of wealth?

Discussion Topics:

The stewardship of wealth in Catholic tradition.

Acts of "charity" as particular duties and charity as a universal motive of the stewardship of wealth.

Social benefits of the investment of money.

Proletarianism in the United States.

Suggested Readings:

Briefs, Goetz, *The Proletariate* (New York: McGraw-Hill Book Co., 1937), Chaps. III, IV, XII.

Bruehl, Charles P., *The Pope's Plan*, pp. 41–90.

Giordani, Igino, *The Social Message of the Early Church Fathers* (New Jersey: St. Anthony Guild Press, 1944), pp. 253–278.

Heilbroner, Robert L., "Who Are the American Poor?" *Harper's Magazine,* June, 1950, pp. 27–33. (Partial reprint in Gayer, Harriss, Spencer, *Basic Economics — A Book of Readings* [New York: Prentice-Hall, 1951], pp. 247–256.)

Kerby, William J., *The Social Mission of Charity* (New York: Macmillan, 1921), Chaps. V, VI, VII, VIII.

Ligutti, Msgr. L., and Rawe, John C., S.J., *Rural Roads to Security* (Milwaukee: The Bruce Publishing Co., 1940), pp. 28–50.

Miller, R., C.Ss.R., *Forty Years After*, pp. 131–139.

Nell-Breuning, O., S.J., *Reorganization of Social Economy*, pp. 148–157.

Ryan, Msgr. J. A., *Distributive Justice*, Chap. 21.

——— *The Christian Doctrine of Property* (New York: The Paulist Press, 1923), N.C.W.C. pamphlet.

Samuelson, Paul A., *Economics, An Introductory Analysis* (New York: McGraw-Hill, 1948), pp. 253–279.

Obligations of Social Justice

SOCIAL JUSTICE AND "NECESSARY" GOODS

THE obligation of social justice with regard to superfluous possessions, as this obligation is derived from the purpose of material goods and the institution of private property, has been stated. It is the obligation of administering those possessions for the good of others who need them. Here the idea of stewardship is patent. It is a dispensation — not merely a distribution — determined in method by the prudent consideration of contingent circumstances. Its whole emphasis is on the assistance of others.

But the obligations of social justice apply to "necessary" goods as well as to superfluous goods. This is clear from the encyclicals. For, according to their teaching previously noted, the obligations of social justice pertain to "non-owners" as well as "owners," by which expressions "wage earners," possessed at most of goods that are termed "necessary," are distinguished from employers or the owners of capital.

With respect to these "necessary" goods, however, the obligations of social justice are quite different from those that affect "superfluous" goods.

When we speak of "necessary" goods, the obvious implication of the word "necessary" is that of the individual utility of the owner — what is needed for the human sustenance of the individual and his family. They represent the necessities of human life and, as such, may, in all good conscience, be devoted to the decent support of the owner and his family. Such a use of necessary goods, as has been said, far from being contrary to social justice, is but a partial realization, through the institution of private property, of the natural destination of material goods, the attainment of which is the aim of social justice.

Therefore, in the words of *Rerum Novarum* (n. 36): "No one, certainly, is obliged to assist others out of what is required for his own necessary use or for that of his family, or even to give to others what he himself needs to maintain his station in life becomingly and decently."

But social justice does affect these necessary goods, not by directing their dispensation but by determining the concrete extent of their "necessary" character.

As is indicated in the preceding quotation from *Rerum Novarum*, and as is found in moral theology textbooks,[1] two classes of "necessary goods" can be distinguished: "absolute" necessities and "conventional" necessities. Absolute necessities are those goods without which the individual and his family would fall into extreme need. They include, therefore, goods necessary for food, clothing, shelter, the proper support and upbringing of children. Conventional necessities embrace those goods required for maintaining one's social position, including, therefore, a greater or smaller number of luxuries. Both together are the material content of what is called a "standard of living."

SOCIAL JUSTICE AND THE STANDARD OF LIVING

This standard of living is not the same for all classes of people. Nor should it be. The nature of society and the differences of individual talents and services necessarily involve differences in material advantages.

Therefore, let it be laid down in the first place that a condition of human existence must be borne with, namely, that in civil society the lowest cannot be made equal with the highest. Socialists, of course, agitate the contrary, but all struggling against nature is vain. There are truly very great and very many natural differences among men. Neither the talents, nor the skill, nor the health, nor the capacities of all are the same, and inequal fortune follows of itself upon necessary inequality in respect to these endowments. And clearly this condition of things is adapted to benefit both individuals and community.[2]

Not only does the standard of living differ between different classes, but, as is also evident, there is no single, fixed standard of living that is universally associated with any particular class. From country to country it will vary in corresponding classes of people. A radio is hardly looked upon as a luxury by the families of workingmen in the United States; it would be included in their "conventional" necessities. Even television sets might be considered by some as belonging to the same category. In less favored lands, however, the possession of such items would be an extraordinary luxury for the working class.

"Conventional necessities" are neither mechanically determined nor defined *a priori*. A standard of living is a cultural and social concept,[3] which depends on the economic resources of a country and on the philosophy which governs the use of those resources and the distribution of income. It is determined for a working man by the wage he receives, by which that distribution is effected in his regard.

It is precisely with this philosophy of distribution and its consequent determination of living standards that social justice is concerned.

Individualistic economic philosophy assumes and defends the proposition that any possible increase of an individual's income is to be devoted to an increase in that fortunate individual's "standard of living." The concept of "conventional necessities" is an elastic concept that may be expanded with every expansion of income, without regard for the effect it may have on the lives of others.

The general acceptance of this position is due to the prevalent influence of an individualistic and materialistic philosophy of life. But the position itself is not new. As far back as 1679 it was censured in the following condemned proposition of Pope Innocent XI: "It is scarcely possible to find among laymen, even among kings, goods that are superfluous to one's state. Therefore hardly anyone is bound to give alms on the score of possessing such goods."[4]

Such an ever expanding concept of conventional necessities and standard of living is opposed to social justice because, again, material goods are made to serve all men in a manner suited to the dignity of human personality. Social justice demands that "conventional necessities," the "standard of living" of the different classes of society be so adjusted as to allow all, as far as possible, to reach at least that "standard" which is required by the dignity of man.

This demand of social justice regarding the adjusting of the standard of living is contained implicitly in the function of social justice, explicitly acknowledged by Pope Pius XI, in regulating the wage scale.

For, as pointed out, wages determine the living standard of the worker. Here[5] *Quadragesimo Anno* further recalls that the number of those who can obtain that determining wage depends in large measure on the scale of wages, which, therefore, looking to the common good, comes under the control of social justice.

Three considerations presented by the encyclical as guides for the determination of the just wage are familiar to all acquainted with its teaching. The wage, first of all, must be sufficient for the support of the worker and his family.[6]

This is not a demand of social justice but of commutative justice. Social justice, as has been noted before, is regulative of the whole economic order in this respect, enabling the fulfillment of this duty of commutative justice.

The second consideration is that of the condition of each particular business.[7] Here, ruinous wage demands are condemned as unjust, and principles are given for the solution of the practical difficulty confronting those businesses unable, for one reason or another, to pay the living wage.

SCALE OF WAGES

The common economic welfare of the whole people is the third factor, and this in virtue of social justice. Social justice commands that wages be determined with a view to providing the maximum employment possible. It ordains not only that wages should not be too low, but also that the wages of some should not be so high as to exhaust the economic system, cause unemployment, and thus prevent others from obtaining, through employment and wages, the necessities of human life.

> To lower or raise wages unduly, with a view to private profit, and with no consideration of the common good, is contrary to Social Justice, which demands that by concerted planning and good will such a scale of wages be set up, if possible, as to offer to the greatest number opportunities of employment and of securing for themselves suitable means of livelihood.[8]

No workingman would object to *Quadragesimo Anno's* first point in determination of wages. A living family wage has long been the object of unionism. Nor would many be opposed to the encyclical's second proposition. Only blind fanaticism would commit the economic suicide which the ruin of a business entails for labor.

But one can well imagine difficulties that wage earners would have in accepting the third proposition, especially in view of the long, difficult struggle labor has had in the period of industrial capitalism to gain recognition and protection of its fundamental rights.

Hasn't the workingman the right to improve his condition as best he can? Why should the burden of providing jobs for all fall on the working class, which is least able to bear the burden?

Improvement of the condition of the worker is not only affirmed by *Quadragesimo Anno* as a right; it is the goal the encyclical has in view. It does not therefore propose a principle which would defeat that improvement. But an ambition of this kind can be as wrong in its individualism as any corresponding avarice on the part of capital.

Neglect of consideration of the common good on the part of the workingmen is traced by *Quadragesimo Anno*[9] to an infiltration of the a-moral economics of business leaders into the ranks of the wage earning class, to the imitation of the "apparent success" of those who, "solely concerned with adding to their own wealth . . . sought their own selfish interests above all things." It would be labor's attempt to get all the traffic will bear.

Sympathetic as one may be for the cause of labor, "the obvious truth is that in labor, especially hired labor, as in ownership, there is a social as well as a personal or individual aspect to be considered."[10] It must, therefore, assume certain social duties, one of which is the modification of its wage demands in line with the purpose of the whole economic system of which it is a part, namely, the securing "for all and each those goods which the wealth and resources of nature, technical achievement and social organization of economic affairs can give."[11] Opportunities for improvement of their state in life is a good which social justice demands should be offered to *all*.

Nor does this place the whole burden on the shoulders of

labor. If social justice demands that the income of the wage earning group be adjusted to provide full employment, *a fortiori* the incomes of those in a higher economic bracket must be accommodated to this same end. The section of the encyclical under discussion expressly mentions both workers and managers (*operarios officialesque*).[12] It further mentions in this same connection that a reasonable proportion between different salaries (*salaria*) should be maintained.[13]

Stress has been placed on the regulation of the wages of the working man because it best illustrates the fact that "necessary" as well as "superfluous" goods come within the sphere of social justice. Such emphasis by no means implies restriction. Granted the differences in station in life between directors of an enterprise and workers, social justice will demand of both a proportionate adjustment of income and standard of living in view of this purpose of providing a human standard for all members of society.

Concrete determination of relative standards of living in accordance with social justice will have many practical difficulties. It cannot be determined by one individual or by any few. It must be based on the economy as a whole. It requires collaborative organization of all the various branches and elements of economic life. It calls for a far more intimate and trusting relationship between labor and management than present-day collective bargaining knows. Without these it is impossible to come to a positive determination.

Yet, negatively, it is possible to point out instances of the violation of social justice in this respect. Cases of disproportionate returns effecting unemployment are not difficult to find. A typical case, based on fact, would be that of a corporation in which four directors would each receive a yearly income (including "salary," "bonuses," and expense accounts) amounting to one hundred and fifty thousand dollars a year. In the same corporation the majority of the labor force would get a wage of about two thousand dollars. If a poor year comes along, three or four hundred workers are laid off. The remainder continue at their jobs with their usual rate of pay; the directors are able to maintain their accustomed income.

A natural and Christian sense of what is right rebels against such a situation. It is wrong. But does the case involve a violation of charity alone? Is it true that the directors, who have made the decision and voted their own salaries, are free of any *injustice* as long as they continue to pay the still employed workers a living wage?

There may be no violation of commutative justice here, but the teaching of *Quadragesimo Anno* with regard to the regulation of salaries in view of maximizing employment opportunities certainly seems to indicate a violation of justice — of social justice.

At this point it is suggested that none of the preceding is written in opposition to what has been called "traditional doctrine." Here an attempt is being made merely to indicate an evolution of that doctrine which papal teaching seems to require. The latter emphasizes, in contrast with the former, the duties attached to property rather than the right itself. Whereas the textbooks will devote seven or eight pages to a discussion of the duties of owners, and a hundred or more to the right, its violation and the matter of restitution, *Quadragesimo Anno* passes briefly over the right of ownership itself, almost assuming it as something clear and certain, and concerns itself at great length with the social aspect of property, its limitations, and duties.

It is naturally understandable that there should be this inversely proportionate treatment. The textbooks must cover the whole field of property relationships; the encyclical is devoted to the correction of excesses in the use of property. But the impression remains that the considerations indicated in the papal documents point out a line of development which should be pursued to accommodate the principles of ownership to modern economic realities.

PLANT AND FACTORY OWNERSHIP

One other such line of development would be in the treatment of the ownership of large capital equipment — of factories and production plants — on which the livelihood of a number of individual workers depends.

Such property cannot be classed as "superfluous," in the usual understanding of the term. This seems to imply income or liquid assets which the owner "spends" or "expends" without curtailment of his manner of living. A man's business enterprise is not such; it is in a true sense "necessary." On it and its prosperity his own livelihood depends.

Furthermore, the ownership of such modern industrial plants is, as a rule, not individual but corporate ownership. Much can be said by way of debate on the relative merit of this type of ownership as compared with a distributist system; but the point here is that, granted the fact, the distinction heretofore mentioned between superfluous goods and necessary goods, on which the duties of "wealth" have been chiefly determined, is inapplicable in determining the duties of the "owner."

Yet the social aspect of such property is evident. The influence of the factory in the modern industrial system on the common good cannot be compared with that of the tools of the independent artisan. The industrial plant is the means of livelihood of hundreds or perhaps thousands, not merely of one. "Strikes," "layoffs," "shutdowns" — expressions which today are synonyms for social suffering — are words which would have been meaningless to St. Thomas when he enunciated the doctrine of the stewardship of wealth.

Consequently, it would seem inadequate to attempt to define the duties of the modern factory owner, individual or corporate, in terms of the obligations of individual producers of a nonindustrial system. There will be duties of "stewardship" over and above those of paying a just wage and charging a just price. The economic welfare of the whole community is vitally affected by the administration of these instruments of industrial production. Social justice, looking to this administration, will impose new duties in view of these circumstances.

RELOCATION OF PLANTS

One instance of such duties of social justice would seem to be involved in the question of relocating plants, of moving factories from one section of the country to another with the sole purpose of maintaining profits for the owner.

Admittedly there can be reasons which would necessitate relocation and which would not necessarily be due to any fault on the part of the "owners." An inequitable tax program could force a firm to give up. A tariff policy might do the same. Unjust competition can close the market to an honest producer.

Such possibilities are acknowledged by *Quadragesimo Anno,* and the blame for the resulting situation is fixed: "(But) if the business in question is not making enough money to pay the workers an equitable wage because it is being crushed by unjust burdens or forced to sell its products at less than a just price, those who are thus the cause of the injury are guilty of a grave wrong. . . ."[14]

Unquestionably, the "grave wrong" here mentioned is a violation of social justice. For, in the preceding section in which the obligation of paying a family wage is discussed, the elimination of those circumstances which make the payment of such a wage impossible is stated to be the task of social justice. If fathers of families cannot receive a wage large enough to meet ordinary family needs under existing circumstances, "Social justice demands that changes be introduced as soon as possible whereby such a wage will be assured to every adult workingman."

And even with regard to the employer himself, who is the victim of this unjust pressure, the language of the encyclical indicates obligations toward his workers which seem to go beyond the obligations of charity alone. The decisions to be made in such a case are not one-sided affairs. "Both workers and employers" must "strive with united strength and counsel to overcome the difficulties and obstacles." And this mutual effort should also mark the final consideration "if matters come to an extreme crisis," and there is question of a complete shutdown.

There is no implication here of an equal right of workers with employers in the disposition of capital equipment. They are not "partners" in the enterprise. And as Pope Pius XII later pointed out when disputes about comanagement arose, labor has no title to economic joint management based on the nature of the wage contract, nor on the nature of an enterprise, nor on the human equality of wage earners and employers.[15]

But it should be noted that the papal statements on this matter, while excluding unlimited economic codetermination based on any of these titles, do leave the way open to some kind of joint responsibility in economic decisions — that kind which seems to be implied necessarily in the papal plan of "Occupational Organization" — based on the common welfare. Such economic codetermination would be not at the plant level, wherein the relationship between employer and worker is governed by the wage contract, but at the occupational level, wherein public economic law, based on the common responsibility of all for the national economy, could limit the freedom of economic decisions of owners. It is suggested that the decision to relocate plants would be among these.

In view of all this, any strict right of commutative justice on the part of the workers to a voice in such a decision of relocation is to be rejected. Similarly, failing the existence of any statute of law, the owner is not bound in legal justice to share his decision. But the strongly commended mutuality of the decision does seem to imply that considerations of the common welfare restrict the complete independence of the owner, in these circumstances, in the disposition of his property. Such a restriction would fall under the virtue of social justice according to the previously indicated analysis of that virtue.

However this may be in the case of "enforced" removal, and whatever may be the obligation imposed by social justice to a joint decision, it seems certain that relocation for the sole purpose of maintaining profit for the owner would be a violation of social justice.

Let a supposition be made of a factory located in a small mill town. Ten per cent of the population of this town depends on it for employment. The economic health of the whole town is likewise dependent on it. It has been a landmark in the town for generations. The factory in its turn has built its success on the labor of generations of the townsfolk.

The labor force is not exorbitant in its wage demands. The company still clears enough to cover costs, maintenance, and necessary improvements, and to guarantee some profit for the owners. But this last, due to increased costs in both material and labor, is not what it used to be. Removal of the plant to another section where labor will be cheaper will restore those former profits.

Given all these conditions, what moral considerations

would affect this decision? Negatively, there would not be an obligation of commutative justice on the owners to keep their mill in production at its present site. Their rights of ownership give them the power of complete disposal as far as commutative justice is concerned. But commutative justice does not exhaust the ground of moral obligation.

Positively, charity would certainly urge continuance of the factory. And, beyond this, social justice would seem to prohibit its removal. Relocation, in these circumstances, would seem to be a practice that comes under the censure placed on individualistic capitalism by *Quadragesimo Anno,* precisely as a violation of social justice. Capitalism, the encyclical teaches, "is not of its own nature vicious. But it does violate right order when capital hires workers, that is, the non-owning working class, with a view to and under such terms that it directs business and even the whole economic system according to its own will and advantage, scorning the human dignity of the workers, the social character of economic activity and social justice itself, and the common good."[16]

The stewardship of wealth, social justice, and its concern with the common economic good limit the moral freedom of the owner. The obligation of social justice, of using one's property to serve the common use of all men, is here concretized and determined, by reason of economic and municipal ties, in favor of this particular community in which the supposed factory is located. Social justice, like charity, begins at home.

All property has a social aspect according to which the obligations of social justice are imposed. But in this case the social aspect of the property in question is determined and accentuated to such an extent, the common economic good of the community is affected to such a degree, that the obligation to provide for the continuance of the plant seems to be the clear dictate of the rational stewardship of wealth.

RIGHT OF WORKING

Does this opinion modify, in any way, the traditional teaching with regard to the "right of working"? If it is true that social justice obliges to the maintenance of the factory, is it not also true — or is this not the equivalent of saying — that the owners are obliged to supply jobs to the people of the town? Does this contradict the distinction in this matter, found in the manuals of moral theology, between the "right of working," which is admitted, and the "right to demand that another supply work," which is denied?[17]

As in previous questions discussed, the present exposition does not in any way deny commonly accepted doctrine but merely suggests certain tentative developments of that doctrine which seem to be founded on the concept of social justice.

Vermeersch[18] describes the "right to work" in the following terms: "The right to work gainfully is no less inviolable than the right to cultivate one's land and sell the fruits thereof. But just as this latter right does not entail any duty of justice whereby others would be bound to buy, so there is no duty of justice in others of hiring labor; nor can anyone, except by reason of contract made, demand that another furnish him with the opportunity to work."

Here, the right to work, like the right to cultivate one's own property with which it is compared, is a strict right of commutative justice. The obligation which is denied as corresponding to this right would likewise be an obligation of commutative justice. In other words, no one can claim from any particular person a right to a determined job.

But this does not deny the obligation which an owner of property will have to the community at large — the obliga-

tion of using his property in such a way as to benefit all.
Such would be an obligation, not of commutative, but of
social justice.

What that use will be in the concrete is determined by
the circumstances of each case, as has been noted before.
In general, the provision, made to the community, of gainful
employment, so strongly recommended by *Quadragesimo
Anno* as an apt means of fulfilling the duties attached to
property, is an obvious and normal social use of property.

In a particular case, as in the present supposition, the
stake that the community at large has in the employment
furnished by the factory, the economic disturbance which
would result from its removal, the fact that the situation
does not entail an initial choice of means in using property
but of the continuance of a long existing institution, all
seem to make the provision of employment a duty owed
not to any individual but to the community itself.

The owner may dispose of his property. He may sell
it to others. He may reorganize, reconvert. Any number
of economic decisions are his. But any decision which would
close off this source of economic life to the community
merely for the sake of private profit would be a violation
of the social duties of property — a violation of social justice.

NATURAL RESOURCES

Another modern problem of property involving social
justice is that of the use of natural resources. One author
presents the case this way:

> Much more serious is the fact that Americans have destroyed
> primary natural resources . . . This conduct is contrary to
> any standards we have reason to approve . . . It is as clearly
> as anything against God's will, if we are in any important
> matter God's stewards . . .

Considering what we do in many states. In Illinois we allow strip mining. This means that the soil, which otherwise might be used for the next hundred years and the next hundred thousand years, is permanently destroyed in order to get quick profits. The standard used is easily seen, and also the immorality. Iowa, Kentucky, Minnesota, Ohio, Indiana, and, without a doubt, other states have allowed the same antihuman action. Some of the topsoil destroyed is only three or four inches deep; nevertheless, it belongs to man, and no king or pope or profit-seeker has the right to destroy it . . .

Favoring this destruction is the argument that a) we must leave man totally free in everything, and b) it is this freedom which has enabled us to develop resources to such a peak.

The reply is that a freedom exercised at the cost of people's good and at the cost of national and international good is a freedom that man may not exercise and yet remain within the bounds of morality. Such a freedom of action may be tolerated only in an emergency. I may not do in the name of freedom, enterprise, and profit the type of act that is sure ultimately to weaken my nation and make it extremely difficult, if not impossible, for people to live. . . .[19]

Father Ward does not use the term "social justice," but his example affords an excellent illustration of that virtue. Here, as he indicates, a right is involved — a right of mankind. The topsoil destroyed (as all primary natural resources) in a true sense "belongs to man, and no king or pope or profiteer has the right to destroy it."

But this is a statement in which the words used are open to misinterpretation. The words, "belongs" and "right," need further explanation. They must be understood in such a way as to exclude the error, discussed in Chapter Four, of those extremists who condemned every misuse of property as a violation of commutative justice. To repeat the words of *Quadragesimo Anno:*[20] "(But) the duty of owners to use their property only in a right way does not come under this type of justice, but under other virtues, obligations of which cannot be enforced by legal action."

Requirements of the common good, in this case of the use of natural resources, could well necessitate the imposition of positive limitations on property rights. But, barring any such legislation of positive law, and, of course, supposing that there is no invasion of the property of another, the owner of the resources in question remains within the bounds of commutative justice in any use he makes of his property. *As far as commutative justice is concerned,* the right of private ownership extends even to the act of the destruction of one's property. In other words, as far as the disposition of the juridical order is concerned, such an act would be "valid" and would not be subject to prosecution; but it could still be an "illicit" act, one which would not "remain within the bounds of morality." And this is the explicit point made by Father Ward.

To say, therefore, that "no king or pope or profiteer has the right to destroy" the topsoil, does not imply that such destruction is a violation of a right of commutative justice. The right that is violated by the selfish destruction of natural resources is a right of "mankind"; it is the right that all men have to demand that the material goods of the world should be managed and used for the common good of mankind. This is a right, not of commutative justice, but of social justice. Natural resources "belong to man" not in the sense of excluding private ownership, but in the sense that they exist for the use and service of all men. The owners of these resources have an obligation, as "God's stewards," to administer their property in such a way as to enable it to serve this purpose. This is the obligation of social justice.

SPECULATION

As a last topic, among many that might be suggested, for the application of this concept of social justice, there is the matter of speculation on the financial markets — on the stock and commodity exchanges. Here is an area of economic activity with regard to which moral teaching often leaves much to be desired.

It is not uncommon to dismiss this matter with a recapitulation of the principles which govern the liceity of gambling. The fact of the relevance of the markets to the common economic good and the consequent social repercussion of speculative operations in them is rather neglected. Even where the danger to the common economic good is mentioned as a vitiating circumstance, this observation receives minor recognition.[21] Yet precisely because of these considerations it seems that speculation on the exchanges should not be judged merely in the light of those principles which pertain to other forms of gambling.

This is the attitude which runs through the more comprehensive treatment of the subject given by Messner[22] and Muller.[23] The position of both of these authors is expressed in summary by Messner: "Speculation is ethically justified when it fulfills a useful function in the economic process, and ethically reprehensible when it is harmful in this respect."[24] Specification of this ethical reprehension would place it primarily under the head of social justice. The social economic process is always a determinant of the moral quality of speculation. Other factors which are decisive of the morality of gambling in general — obligations, e.g., to family and creditors, or the use of fraud, or the growth of avarice — will, of course, enter into consideration; but in this type of "gambling" the prime and universal criterion is the common economic good.[25]

The social implications of transactions on the exchanges

are clear. Besides providing a widespread, ready means of investment and purchase, the markets act (ideally) as a barometer of economic activity. Here a concentrated picture of supply and demand is given, bringing several benefits to the national economy: the markets thus become regulative of the price level; they influence the flow of funds into various enterprises; they furnish businessmen with the knowledge necessary to plan their activities with prudence.

The social evil of speculation consists in the frustration of these purposes on which the health of the whole economic process depends. And this is the evil which *Quadragesimo Anno* condemns in its criticism of market practices.

> The easy gains that a market unrestricted by any law opens to everybody attracts large numbers to buying and selling goods, and they, their one aim being to make quick profits with the least expenditure of work, raise or lower prices by their uncontrolled business dealings so rapidly according to their own caprice and greed that they nullify the wisest forecasts of producers.[26]

All speculation, however, does not have this frustrating effect. The use, for example, of the futures markets by a producer or manufacturer will be a kind of speculation which at the same time is a prudent insurance against loss. Speculative activity can have the effect of reducing the violence of price changes. Speculation by dealers providing a continuous market for securities decreases the risk for producers who are thus assured of capital invested.

But all these legitimate forms of speculation suppose a special knowledge of the market, an experience, and training which enables one to know the probable influences that will affect it, and a study of the actual state of the economy which is directed to the foretelling of likely economic trends. Apart from such knowledge, study, and appraisal, speculation is a "gamble" that endangers the common good.

The morality of a concrete act of speculation, therefore, turns first of all on the type of person who speculates. And this would seem to be the reason why the encyclical complains that the market is open "to everybody." Manufacturers, producers, professional dealers in the market may engage in the act legitimately (understanding, from what has been said, that even in the case of these agents speculation which involves fraud will be illicit). But speculation on the part of the general public, with no special knowledge of the market, looking for "easy gains" from the variation of quoted prices, can be justified with difficulty, if at all.

NOTES FOR CHAPTER FIVE

1. Vermeersch, *Theol. Moralis*, Vol. II, n. 96, 2; Noldin, II, n. 90, 2.
2. *Rerum Novarum*, n. 26.
3. Richard E. Mulcahy, S.J., *The Economics of Heinrich Pesch* (New York: Henry Holt and Co., 1952), p. 53.
4. Denzinger-Bannwart, *Enchiridion Symbolorum*, n. 1162.
5. *Quad. Anno*, n. 74.
6. *Ibid.*, n. 71.
7. *Ibid.*, n. 72.
8. *Ibid.*, n. 74.
9. *Ibid.*, nn. 133–135.
10. *Ibid.*, n. 69.
11. *Ibid.*, n. 75.
12. *Ibid.*, n. 74.
13. *Ibid.*, n. 75.
14. *Ibid.*, n. 72.
15. Cf. Address to Catholic Employers, May 7, 1949, *The Catholic Mind*, July, 1949, pp. 445–448; and, Address to the Cath. International Congress for Social Studies and Social Action, June 3, 1950, *The Catholic Mind*, Aug., 1950, pp. 507–510.
16. N. 101.
17. Noldin, *Theol. Moralis*, II, n. 69.
18. *Quaestiones de Justitia*, n. 440.
19. Leo R. Ward, C.S.C., *Christian Ethics* (St. Louis, Mo.: B. Herder Book Co., 1952), pp. 133–135.
20. N. 47.
21. Cf. Noldin, *Summa Theologiae Moralis*, Vol. II, n. 633, a.
22. *Social Ethics*, p. 851 ff.
23. *Notes D'Economie Politique* (Paris: Editions Spes, 1938), p. 359 ff.
24. *Op. cit.*, p. 853. This is a moral judgment merely from the social aspect of speculation. As is clear from the author, other considerations can modify the moral character of speculation. The point here made is that

over and above these other considerations, the social effect of the act must always be weighed.

25. This would add determination to the moral quality of illicit speculation, as against the assertion of Noldin (*op. cit.,* n. 633, c) that in speculation "the sin is not of one determined species but can belong to several together." The other specific types of malice he enumerates may indeed be present, but illicit speculation would always involve social justice.

26. N. 132.

Chapter Five

STUDY AIDS

Review Questions:

Do the obligations of social justice apply to the ownership of "necessary" goods?

Are men obliged to assist others out of goods necessary for themselves or their families?

What are "absolute" necessities? What are "conventional" necessities?

What is meant by a "standard of living"?

Should this standard be the same for all?

What considerations determine the standard of living?

Does social justice determine absolutely what this standard should be?

What is the demand of social justice in this matter?

Where does the encyclical *Quadragesimo Anno* implicitly treat of this point?

What are the three factors, enumerated by *Quadragesimo Anno,* which determine the just wage?

How are wages to be regulated by social justice?

Has labor, no less than ownership, a social as well as an individual aspect?

Are the wages of labor the only income subject to the regulations of social justice?

Why is it that the ownership of modern industrial plants does not exactly fit the traditional classification of "necessary" and "superfluous" goods?

How does the social aspect of modern capital ownership compare with preindustrial capital ownership?

Can the relocation of industrial plants be justified on the part of owners in some cases?

Has labor a strict right to share in such decisions?

What considerations restrict the independence of the owners in such cases?

Is social justice included in these considerations?

Do concrete economic and community ties determine the general duties of the stewardship of wealth?

Has man a strict right of working for a living?

Does this right impose an obligation of commutative justice on any other particular individual to supply him with a job?

Can there be an obligation in social justice of maintaining job opportunities for the common good?

In what sense do natural resources belong to all men?

Does this exclude private ownership of these resources?

How does the distinction between the right of ownership and the use of property (cf. Chap. Three) apply to this matter?

Are speculation on the market and private gambling exactly the same?

How would speculation be contrary to social justice?

Discussion Topics:
The social aspect of labor
The wage rate and its effect on employment
The effect of unionization on the location of industry
Taxation policies and industry
Causes of the market crash of 1929

Suggested Readings:
Baerwald, Friedrich, *Fundamentals of Labor Economics* (New York: Declan X. McMullen Co., 1947), Chaps. 3 and 21.

Burck, G., and Silberman, C., "What Caused the Depression?" *Fortune,* Feb., 1955.

George, Gordon, S.J., "The Family Living Wage," *Social Order,* Nov., 1948, p. 385, and Jan., 1949, p. 23.

Hansen, A. H., *Economic Policy and Full Employment* (New York: McGraw-Hill, 1947), pp. 152–160.

Harris, Seymour E., *The Economics of New England* (Cambridge: Harvard Univ. Press, 1952), pp. 171–177, 183–202.

Harriss, C. Lowell, *The American Economy* (Chicago: R. D. Irwin, Inc., 1953), pp. 879–914.

Hicks, J. R., "Wage Regulation and Unemployment," in Bakke and Kerr, *Unions, Management and the Public* (New York: Harcourt, Brace, 1948), pp. 780–783.

Lester, R. A., "Southern Wage Differentials: Developments, Analysis and Implications," *Southern Economic Journal,* Vol. XIII, Apr., 1947), pp. 386–394.

Messner, J., *Social Ethics,* pp. 759–769, 851–861.

Schumpeter, J. A., "The Decade of the Twenties," *American Economic Review,* Vol. XXXVI, Supplement, May, 1946, pp. 1–10.

Seidman, Joel, *Union Rights and Union Duties* (New York: Harcourt, Brace and Co., 1943), Chaps. 1, 3, 5.

Shister, Joseph, *Economics of the Labor Market* (New York: Lippincott, 1949), pp. 475–488, 530–542.

Social Justice and Social Organization

NECESSITY OF ORGANIZATION

AN EVIDENT corollary of the preceding reflections on the nature of social justice is the necessity of social organization. The realization of social justice is not to be accomplished by isolated individual effort; it can only be the result of social co-operation. Social justice places duties on individuals, but the conditions enabling its practice are so many and diverse that, without the organization of social effort, the individual remains impotent.

Social justice, as has been noted, demands changes in the socioeconomic order which will assure a family wage to every adult workingman. The encyclical *Divini Redemptoris* specifies these changes[1] when it directs that institutions must be organized to prevent competition incompatible with the fair treatment of workers, since individual employers are all too frequently helpless to insure justice by themselves. A further demand of social justice, also already indicated, is a right proportion in wages and salaries which will bring about the maximum spread of employment. Essential to this proportion is "a right proportion in the prices at which the goods are sold that are produced by the various occupations, such as agriculture, manufacturing and others."[2] And the encyclical goes on immediately to add that "if all these relations are properly maintained, the various occupations will combine and coalesce into, as it were, a single body and like the members of the body mutually aid and complete one another." Social organization and the realization of social justice go hand in hand.

Social justice calls for the redistribution of wealth.[3] This is perhaps the cardinal economic reform proposed by *Quadragesimo Anno,* being a synonym for the redemption of the proletariate which is described by the encyclical[4] as "the goal which Our Predecessor declared must necessarily be sought."

But this redistribution does not mean merely a mechanical redivision of existing wealth. Social justice, as proposed by the encyclicals, is not a dissector of a static economic stockpile; it is the directing principle of a dynamic economic process whose purpose is the ever increasing satisfaction of the material needs of all — the advancement of the whole people "to that happier and fuller condition of life which, when wisely cared for, is not only no hindrance to virtue but helps it greatly."[5]

Hence the redistribution which is envisaged must be thought of in terms of this process. The energy and motivation needed for a continued and enlarged production of goods must be safeguarded, while the participation in its benefits is ever widened. And this increased share, in its turn, must represent an increased contribution to the economic process. Redistribution of wealth thus involves principally a better distribution of economic opportunity, both personal and geographic.

The detailed means which will effectuate such a program cannot be determined from a consideration of ethical principles alone. "The laws of economics, as they are termed, being based on the very nature of material things and on the capacities of the human mind and body, determine the limits of what productive human effort cannot, and what it can attain in the economic field and by what means."[6] As in any case of the application of the natural law, so here, the determination of the means by which this necessary end is to be obtained supposes an experimental knowledge of all those contingent realities which affect the practicability of any determinate proposal.

Given these limitations, however, it is evident that the purpose of social justice can be attained only through the concerted efforts of all who are engaged in the economic process. The right ordering of economic life cannot be founded on the antagonisms of either class warfare or unrestricted competition. The conflict which has characterized the atomization of society since the prevalence of individualism must be replaced by the co-operation of an organized social body. At the same time, this necessary organization must avoid the danger of stifling initiative or of substituting for economic anarchy an equally noxious political regimentation.

It is this vital problem of social organization which occupies such a central position in the teaching of *Quadragesimo Anno* that it gives to the encyclical its English title: "On Reconstructing the Social Order."

THREE ESSENTIAL REFORMS

Three reforms are urged by the encyclical, all of which are essential to the solution of the "Social Question." The first of these, and the most fundamental in the sense that without it "all our efforts" will "be wasted and our house be builded not on rock but on shifting sand,"[7] is a moral reform, a renewal of the Christian spirit. This means a renovation of the Christian concept of the meaning and purpose of human life, which will put the purposes of economic activity in their proper place.[8] More particularly it calls for a renovation of the spirit of charity and social justice which will motivate mutual collaboration and a more social use of property.[9]

The second reform is economic. It consists in a more equitable distribution of wealth[10] and the "redemption" of the nonowning workers through the acquisition of some modest property.[11]

And, finally, there must be a reform of institutions, which reform will affect both the State and the various industries and professions that constitute the socioeconomic community.[12] The latter must be reconstituted as self-governing,[13] co-operating,[14] members of the social body,[15] combining men according to the common social function of their particular occupation; the State must return to its proper function of *promoting* the common good, by stimulating, protecting, and co-ordinating these occupational associations which effect it.[16]

Though mentioned here in the last place, this institutional reorganization of society is not to be considered of least importance in bringing about the realization of social justice. On the contrary, Pope Pius XII was later to call the section of *Quadragesimo Anno* which contains the social policy embodying the idea of an occupational, corporative order of the whole economy the "chief part" of the encyclical.[17]

In the words of the encyclical itself: "Complete cure will not come until this opposition has been abolished and well-ordered members of the social body — Industries and Professions — are constituted in which men may have their place, not according to the position each has in the labor market, but according to the respective social functions which each performs."[18]

The essential gravity of this social reorganization was repeated again by Pope Pius XI in the encyclical on Atheistic Communism:

If, therefore, we consider the whole structure of economic life, as we have already pointed out in our Encyclical Quadragesimo Anno, the reign of justice and charity in social-economic relations can only be achieved when professional and interprofessional organizations, based on the solid foundations of Christian teaching, constitute, under forms adapted to different places and circumstances, what used to be called guilds.[19]

So necessary and intimate is the relationship between social organization and social justice in papal teaching that Ferree, in his study of the virtue, makes "the organization of human acts into social media and institutions (social habits) of which society is composed" the "material cause" of social justice.[20]

The present analysis differs from that of Ferree with regard to the object of social justice (assuming Ferree's "material cause" to be what, in the terminology of St. Thomas, is the "object" of a virtue), as is evident from what has gone before.[21] But this is not to minimize the importance of the organization itself. The act of organizing will at times be commanded by social justice, not because that act is the object of the virtue, but because the social use of property cannot be realized without organization. This relationship between social justice and social organization is illuminated by the evident order that obtains between the three reforms sought by *Quadragesimo Anno*. The economic reform is the end which is sought. The moral reform is the motivating cause. The institutional reform is a *conditio sine qua non*. And since social justice occupies a principal place in the moral reform, social reorganization becomes a necessary demand of that virtue.

Such professional organizations, however, are not to be conceived merely as utilitarian expedients. They are, in a sense, institutions of natural law. "For under nature's guidance it comes to pass that just as those who are joined together by nearness of habitation establish towns, so those who follow the same industry or profession — whether in the economic or other field — form guilds or associations, so that many are wont to consider these self-governing organizations, if not essential, at least natural to civil society."[22]

Nature, on the other hand, does not determine the concrete form that these associations will take. That is to be "adapted to different places and circumstances."[23] Even as in the case of political society which grows from the nature of man but whose form is freely determined by men, so in the "guilds" of the various industries and professions "men are free to choose whatever form they please, provided that proper regard is had for the requirements of justice and the common good."[24]

Thus in the institutional reform of society along the lines of professions and industries, two different aspects can and must be considered. The first is that of the social philosophy which requires such organization. The second is that of the economic and social feasibility of any concrete actuation. The encyclicals are concerned with the first of these; the second, dependent as it is upon the existing variable conditions of place, time, cultural development, and resources, is left to the decision of the members themselves of the professions.

Three regulative philosophical concepts require the organization of "Industries and Professions" as proposed by *Quadragesimo Anno:* the social function of economic activity; the organic nature of society; and the principle of subsidiarity in social life.

THE SOCIAL FUNCTION OF ECONOMIC ACTIVITY

The idea of economic activity as a social function is the root of socioeconomic reorganization. Economic activity in society is not merely a means of enriching those engaged in it, either at the expense of others or merely disregarding them. Like the property it utilizes and the labor which effects it, it has a social as well as an individual aspect. It has a social function of supplying commodities and services to the community.

In other lines of human activity, the social function is clearly seen. The practice of medicine, of law, the vocation of teaching — all the so-called "professions" — while providing a living for the individuals engaged in them, all imply a dedication to the service of society. But in economic activity this social ideal has been lost. It is conceived rather as a "competitive struggle," ruled by the "free competition of forces,"[25] the motive and norm of which is individual profit.

As a result, our present society is "in a violent condition and is unstable and uncertain," as *Quadragesimo Anno* points out, being "founded on classes with divergent aims and hence opposed to one another and therefore inclined to enmity and strife."[26] The employer wants higher prices and lower costs; the employed want lower prices and higher wages; individual enterprises within an industry do everything to capture the market from the others. Each class and concern is engaged in the promotion of its own private good.

Quite evidently the unity necessary for that mutual supplementation which the social nature of man requires cannot be founded on this opposition. Nor can the co-operation needed for the proper ordering of economic life be expected from the unrestricted competition which arises from it. A strong bond which will unite the members of economic society must be found. Or, rather, the bond which does so unite them must be allowed to be effective.

For actually there is a bond which unites capital and labor. It is the social function which is the purpose of every branch of economic and industrial life. "This unifying force is present — in the producing of goods or the rendering of services — in which the employers and employees of an identical Industry or Profession collaborate jointly."[27]

From top to bottom of any branch of economic life there is a common interest: the production of a particular type of goods — autos, shoes, electrical equipment, farm products — for social use. And by reason of this common interest, all the members of any branch of the economy belong to a unified group, variously called a "professional" group, a "vocational" group, an "occupational" group.

> The community is supplied with various commodities and services by particular groups in society, such as the teaching profession, shoemakers, publishers, provision merchants, the agricultural community, the motor industry. Their members are bound together within the framework of social cooperation by their social functions, and thus form an occupational group to meet the demands of the members of the great society.[28]

In the social function of the occupational group there is, therefore, a natural principle of social organization which "is above the distinction between employers and workers."[29] This does not, however, deny the distinction. The existence of social classes is not an evil. It is their antisocial antagonism that is condemned. As "classes," capital and labor have their own proper interests; but by reason of their common task they also constitute, within each industry, an "order," the expression used by *Quadragesimo Anno* to describe the "vocational group." It is only within a structure of "orders" that the complementary nature of the different "classes" can be realized.

The words "class" and "order" express perfectly the contrast which the encyclical wants to convey. The sharp antithesis between these two words, eminently clear in the original text of the encyclical,[30] is lost in the English version. "Industries and Professions" is an authorized translation of the simple word *ordines* found in the Latin text. But the term "industries and professions" contains no philosophical or sociological overtone which, when compared with the meaning of the word "classes," brings out the full significance of their contrast. In the words "orders" and "classes" the significance is pellucid.

A social "class" is, by definition, "a category of persons who share the possession of a similar social status."[31] To speak of different social "classes" is to suggest the ideas of separation, distance, and mutual barriers. Intercommunication between the members of different social classes is not the rule; and often there is positive opposition between them. The social ideals of the "class," "insofar as they discriminate between this class and others, are disruptive of the unity of the total group."[32]

"Order," on the other hand, suggests unity and mutual collaboration. Abstractly, "order" is a harmonious disposition of different things according to some unified plan. Concretely applied to human associations, an "order" is a group of persons striving for a common good. In the unlikely place of his treatise "De Angelis," St. Thomas describes these "orders" of human society:

> A multitude would not be ordered, but confused, if there were not different orders in the multitude. The very notion of hierarchy ("a multitude ordered in one way under the rule of a head"), therefore, requires a diversity of orders. And this diversity of orders is decided by diversity of functions and acts, as it is evident that in one city there are different orders according to different acts; for there is one order of those who judge, another of those who fight, another of those who work in the fields and so forth.[33]

The "orders," therefore, imply union within the group

by reason of a common function, and co-ordination with other groups in the fulfillment of diverse functions. We can speak of "class warfare," but the expression "order warfare" would be absurd. From the same idea of social function there proceed both the inner unity of each occupational group and the further unity of all the groups in the larger civil society.

> This unifying force is present not only in the producing of goods . . . but also in that common good, to achieve which all Industries and Professions together ought, each to the best of its ability, to cooperate amicably. And this unity will be the stronger and more effective, the more faithfully individuals and the Industries and Professions themselves strive to do their work and excel in it.[34]

THE ORGANIC NATURE OF SOCIETY

A structure of society, and a philosophy of society, utterly opposed to both the hitherto prevailing individualistic system and the presently threatening collectivist, is implicit in the "orders." The occupational groups, formed about their various social functions, are the natural units of social co-operation and the component parts of the social body. Society thus becomes, on the analogy of the human body, a moral organism, characterized by what is known as social pluralism and governed by the philosophy which Pesch calls solidarism.

"Solidarism," "pluralism," and "organism" — all are terms describing, each with its own nuance, the "true and genuine social order,"[35] which is the aim of *Quadragesimo Anno's* "reform of institutions." "Solidarism" emphasizes the *unity* of an undivided whole made up of a multiplicity of responsible members,[36] as against the disintegration of individualism. "Pluralism" stresses the *variety* of self-determining parts which coalesce in the unity of the social whole,[37] in opposition to the authoritarian monism of collectivism.

"Organism" underlines the inner principle of common purpose by reason of which the autonomous parts co-operate in the unity of the whole, in contrast to the mechanistic forces which explain social interaction in both individualism and collectivism.

The radical difficulty with the social order, according to *Quadragesimo Anno,* is that social life has entirely lost this organic form: " . . . Things have come to such a pass through the evil of what we have termed 'individualism,' that, following upon the overthrow and near extinction of that rich social life which was once highly developed through associations of various kinds, there remain virtually only individuals and the State."[38]

Conceiving society as a group of competing individuals held together by the external authority of the State, the only function of which is to preserve conditions necessary for free competition, Individualism has eliminated any inner principle of social unity. The State has ceased to be a moral whole made up of heterogeneous parts, each one of which, like the organs of the body, has a definite function to perform, and from whose harmonious co-operation the perfection of the whole results.

The result is a "mass" society so trenchantly contrasted with an authentic human society by Pope Pius XII in his Christmas message of 1944:

> The state is not a distinct entity which mechanically gathers together a shapeless mass of individuals and confines them within a specified territory.
>
> It is and should be in practise the organic and organizing unity of a real people. The people and a shapeless multitude (or as it is called "the masses") are two distinct concepts.
>
> The people lives and moves by its own life energy; the masses are inert of themselves and can only be moved from the outside. The people lives by the fullness of life in the men that

compose it, each of whom — in his proper place and in his own way — is a person conscious of his own responsibility and of his own views.

The masses, on the contrary, waiting for the impulse from outside, become an easy plaything in the hands of anyone who seeks to exploit their instincts and impressions. They are ready to follow, in turn, today this flag, tomorrow another.

From the exuberant life of a true people, an abundant, rich life is diffused in the state and in all its institutions. With a constantly self-renewing vigor, it instills into the citizens the consciousness of their own responsibility, and a true instinct for the common good.[39]

It is to restore society to this "organic unity of a true people" living "by its own life energy" in which each of the men who compose it "is a person conscious of his own responsibility and of his own views," that *Quadragesimo Anno* proposes its institutional reform of the "orders."

In this conception we are not left with "only individuals and the state." Man is not the atomized member of an amorphous collection of similar atomized individuals.

The "orders" restore to autonomous lesser groups within the State their proper responsibility for the attainment of particular ends, and this responsibility shared by all the members of the groups, becomes at once the principle of social unity and the expression of personal dignity.

THE PRINCIPLE OF SUBSIDIARITY IN SOCIAL LIFE

The ideal of the "orders," as also the very purpose of social justice, acknowledges the need of a rational control and direction of economic activity. Harmonization of individual activities in view of the common good, the consideration which holds first place in the "orders"[40] cannot be the mechanical product of the unregulated exercise of those activities. Tendencies to selfish aggrandizement must be socially curbed and ruled.

Competition is a case in point. Competition is recognized by *Quadragesimo Anno* as justified and useful in economic life.[41] It is characterized by the Social Code of Mechlin as one of the "two great stimulants to production,"[42] the other being the prospect of acquiring property. But this admitted competition is qualified by the words "limited" and "lawful." Unlimited competition, callous to the social character of economic life, introduces the law of the jungle into human society, and eventually leads, as history shows, to the destruction of competition itself. By force of events individualistic theory has been compelled to admit this, and has necessarily modified its resistance to public economic control.[43]

But it is at this point that the ultimate bankruptcy of individualism becomes apparent in its inability to institute such control without opening the way to the statism it abhors. Because of the dichotomy it has introduced between individuals and the State, individualism sets the stage for the appearance of the totalitarian State. Big business has meant big — and ever growing — government. There has been only the State to turn to for the amelioration of social evils brought about by unregulated free competition. Hence, in the course of time, the state has enlarged its sphere of action in economic life to such an extent that a real danger of state domination threatens individual liberty.

The reintroduction into social life of the principle of subsidiarity, a principle which is to be realized in the reconstruction of the "orders," is the safeguard against this danger offered by *Quadragesimo Anno's* institutional reform. By reason of this principle a distinction exists between "social" control and "state" control, a distinction which should not be overlooked in the encyclical's complaint of the dissolution of the organic structure of society.

> With a structure of social governance lost (*amissa forma regiminis socialis*) and with the taking over of all the burdens

which the wrecked associations once bore, the State has been overwhelmed and crushed by almost infinite tasks and duties.[44]

The subsidiary character of social activity is rooted in the self-determining, self-responsible nature of the human person. To be a person means to be the responsible agent of one's own perfection. And, consequently, while co-operation in seeking those social ends which are the condition of personal perfection is an obligation of man, that never implies the surrender of his responsibility nor of the right of self-direction which springs from it. Social activity is always complementary activity. Men do not form societies to give themselves up or to be absorbed but to be helped mutually in the obtaining of the common good. The authority of society is derived from the necessity of this common good but it is also determined in subject and limited in extent by this same consideration.

As history abundantly proves, it is true that on account of changed conditions many things which were done by small associations in former times cannot be done now save by large associations. Still, the most weighty principle, which cannot be set aside or changed, remains fixed and unshaken in social philosophy: Just as it is gravely wrong to take from individuals what they can accomplish by their own initiative and industry and give it to the community, so also it is an injustice and at the same time a grave evil and disturbance of right order to assign to a greater and higher association what lesser and subordinate organizations can do. For every social activity ought of its very nature to furnish help to the members of the body social, and never destroy and absorb them.[45]

The supreme authority of the State ought, therefore, to let subordinate groups handle matters and concerns of lesser importance, which would otherwise dissipate its efforts greatly. Thereby the State will more freely, powerfully, and effectively do all those things that belong to it alone because it alone can do them: directing, watching, urging, restraining, as occasion requires and necessity demands. Therefore, those in power should be sure that the more perfectly a graduated order is kept among the various associations, in observance of the principle of "subsidiary function," the stronger social authority and effectiveness will be and the happier and more prosperous the condition of the State.[46]

From these words it is unmistakably clear that the "ordered" social structure proposed by the encyclical is opposed to totalitarianism no less than to individualism. Social control of our modern gigantic economic system is necessary. Effective regulation is essential. But, in the interest of human freedom, this control should come immediately from those engaged in the work of the system, not from the state.

Such social self-control is the aim of the "orders." It is not regimentation or authoritarianism. It is nothing but accountable freedom, such as any freedom must be which hopes to survive.

The complete accord with freedom of this control through vocational groups is borne out, independently of anything the encyclical has to say, by the interesting conclusion reached in the report of the commission set up several years ago to study the freedom of the press. The commission found freedom of the press in danger. Protection of that freedom in the future depends on its being an accountable freedom. Hence, in so far as possible, the press must form itself into an occupational group, similar to that of doctors or lawyers, with its own institutionalized conscience and code of ethics.[47]

The "orders," then, are the lesser groups to whom the care and regulation of their particular functions belong. They are not merely creatures of the state. They enjoy a real, though relative, autonomy: a real autonomy because every function is the source of a responsibility and consequently of a right of self-direction, with which right no other social authority may interfere as long as the responsibility is met; a relative autonomy because all the "orders" are linked together in a supreme unity of order over which the authority of the State presides. The State may thus assist, stimulate, co-ordinate the "orders" but it may not substitute itself for them.

In these principles which the last few pages have been discussing (The Social Function of Economic Activity, The Organic Nature of Society, and The Principle of Subsidiarity) the encyclical proposed the ethical framework of a socioeconomic structure which Messner describes as a "socially integrated democracy." His expression describes the ordered system which social justice requires. It means "a social system in which freedom and order, individual interest and general interest, individual and community, are so correlated that the individual can make profit only if he is also promoting the general interest, and the community can benefit only so long as it respects and promotes the freedom of the individual. In such a correlation lies the essence of the social order."[48]

NOTES FOR CHAPTER SIX

1. N. 53.
2. *Quad. Anno*, n. 75.
3. *Ibid.*, n. 58.
4. *Ibid.*, n. 59.
5. *Ibid.*, n. 75.
6. *Ibid.*, n. 42.
7. *Ibid.*, n. 127.
8. *Ibid.*, n. 136.
9. *Ibid.*, nn. 126 and 127.
10. *Ibid.*, n. 57.
11. *Ibid.*, nn. 59 and 63.
12. *Ibid.*, nn. 77 and 98.
13. *Ibid.*, n. 83
14. *Ibid.*, n. 85.
15. *Ibid.*, n. 90.
16. *Ibid.*, nn. 79 and 80.
17. Address to Italian Catholic Assoc. of Employers, Jan. 31, 1952, *Catholic*

Mind, Sept., 1952, p. 571.

18. *Quad. Anno,* n. 83.
19. *Divini Redemptoris,* n. 54.
20. *The Act of Social Justice,* p. 202.
21. Cf. Chapter Three.
22. *Quad. Anno,* n. 83.
23. *Divini Redemptoris,* n. 54.
24. *Quad. Anno,* n. 86.
25. *Ibid.,* n. 88.
26. *Ibid.,* n. 82.
27. *Ibid.,* n. 84.
28. Messner, *Social Ethics,* pp. 333–334.
29. Pius XII to the Italian Workers, March, 1954, *Catholic Action,* June, 1954, p. 5.
30. *Quad. Anno,* n. 81: — "ut 'classium' oppositarum disceptione superata, concors 'ordinum' conspiratio excitetur et provehatur."
31. N. Timasheff and P. Facey, S.J., *Sociology* (Milwaukee: The Bruce Publishing Co., 1949), p. 104.
32. *Ibid.,* p. 111.
33. *Summa Theol.,* I, q. 108, a. 2; cf. also *Summa Theol.,* III, q. 8, a. 4.
34. *Quad. Anno,* n. 84.
35. *Ibid.,* n. 84.
36. Cf. Mulcahy, *The Economics of Heinrich Pesch,* pp. 163–164.
37. Cf. Messner, *Social Ethics,* p. 140.
38. *Quad. Anno,* n. 78.
39. *Pius XII and Democracy* (Paulist Press, 1945), nn. 21–25.
40. *Quad. Anno,* n. 85.
41. *Ibid.,* n. 88.
42. *A Code of Social Principles,* prepared by International Union of Social Studies, 2nd ed. (Oxford: Catholic Social Guild, 1933), n. 107.
43. Cf. J. A. Schumpeter, *History of Economic Analysis* (Oxford Univ. Press, 1954), p. 761.
44. *Quad. Anno,* n. 78.
45. *Ibid.,* n. 79.
46. *Ibid.,* n. 80.
47. Cf. *A Free and Responsible Press* (Univ. of Chicago Press, 1947).
48. *Social Ethics,* pp. 896–897.

Chapter Six

STUDY AIDS

Review Questions:

Can social justice be realized by isolated individual effort?

What are some of the demands of social justice which require organized effort?

What place does the problem of social organization hold in the teaching of *Quadragesimo Anno?*

What three reforms are urged by *Quadragesimo Anno* as essential to the solution of the "social question"?

In general, how does the "reform of institutions" affect the various industries in their relation to the State?

Are "professional" organizations in any sense "natural" institutions?

Does nature determine their concrete forms?

What principles of social philosophy call for the organization of "industries and professions"?

What is meant by the social function of economic activity?

What does the term "profession" add to the idea of any human activity?

Why has the social ideal of economic activity been lost?

Is there a bond of union between capital and labor?

What is meant by a "vocational" or "occupational" group?

What is the difference between "social classes" and "social orders"?

What is the principle of unity of the "social order"?

What is meant by the organic nature of society?

How is this concept contrasted with the individualistic and collectivist concepts of society?

What is the difference between "the masses" and "a people"?

How do the "orders" restore organic unity to society?

Must economic activity be subject to control?

Does social control of economic activity imply "statism"?

What is the difference between state control and social control?

What is meant by the subsidiary nature of social activity?

On what is the principle of subsidiarity based?

Do the social "orders" possess genuine social authority and autonomy?

What authority belongs to the State according to this principle?

What relationship of individual and community does genuine social order require?

Discussion Topics:

Differences between a moral organism and a physical organism

The principle of subsidiarity

Reconciliation of liberty and authority

Union-Management co-operation

Suggested Readings:

Cronin, J. F., S.S., *Catholic Social Principles,* Chap. VII.

Davenport, R. W., "Enterprise for Everyman," *Fortune*, Jan., 1950, p. 55.
Dempsey, B. W., S.J., "Economic Community," *Social Order*, Vol. V, Apr., 1955, pp. 147–154.
Drummond, W. F., S.J., "Liberty and Authority," *Social Order*, Vol. I, 1951, pp. 249–252.
Kenney, J. F., S.J., "The Principle of Subsidiarity," *American Catholic Sociological Review*, Mar., 1955, pp. 31–36.
Messner, J., *Social Ethics*, pp. 331–355, 196–200.
Mulcahy, R. E., S.J., *The Economics of Heinrich Pesch*, Chap. 7.
Rommen, H., *The State in Catholic Thought*, Chap. IV.
Schmandt, H. J., "State Intervention — When?" *Social Order*, Vol. IV, Dec., 1954, pp. 435–440.
Simon, Yves R., *Nature and Functions of Authority* (Milwaukee: Marquette Univ. Press, 1940).

Bibliography

Antoine, Ch., *Cours D'Economie Sociale*, 6th ed. (Paris: Alcan, 1921).
Aquinas, St. Thomas, *Summa Theologica*, emendata de Rubeis, Billuart et Aliorum notis selectis ornata (Taurini: Marietti, 1932).
——— *Summa Contra Gentiles* seu De Veritate Catholicae Fidei, reimpressio XXII stereotypa (Taurini: Marietti, 1937).
Ares, Richard, S.J., *What Is Corporative Organization?* trans., Thomas P. Fay, S.J. (St. Louis: Central Bureau Press, 1937).
Baerwald, Friedrich, "Social Justice and the Distribution of Wealth," *Thought*, Vol. 10, No. 3, Dec., 1935, p. 480.
Bishops of the Philippines, "Social Justice," Joint Pastoral Letter, May 21, 1949, *The Catholic Mind*, Vol. 47, No. 1041, Sept., 1949, pp. 565–572.
Bishops of Quebec, *The Problem of the Worker*, Joint Pastoral Letter, Feb. 14, 1950 (Montreal: Palm Publishers).
Bishops of the United States, "God's Law: The Measure of Man's Conduct," Statement of Nov. 18, 1951, *The Catholic Mind*, Vol. 50, No. 1070, Feb., 1952, p. 121.
——— "The Dignity of Man," Statement of Nov. 22, 1953, *The Catholic Mind*, Vol. 52, No. 1094, Feb., 1954, p. 123.
Bourke, Vernon J., *Ethics* (New York: Macmillan, 1951).

Bouvier, Emile, S.J., *Guaranteed Annual Wage* (Montreal: Industrial and Labor Publications, 1954).

Brauer, Theodore, "Economic Thought in St. Thomas" in *Thomistic Principles in a Catholic School* by T. Brauer and others (St. Louis: Herder, 1943), pp. 142–183.

Briefs, Goetz A., "Sociological Aspects of Union-Management Cooperation," *Review of Social Economy*, Vol. V, No. 1, June, 1947, pp. 59–68.

Brown, Francis J., *Social Justice in the Modern World*, encyclical letter of Pope Pius XI (*Quadragesimo Anno*) with Outline and Index (Chicago: Outline Press, 1947).

Brown, Leo C., S.J., "Labor-Management Cooperation," *Social Order*, Vol. 1, No. 5, May, 1951, pp. 211–223.

Brucculeri, A., S.J., "La Giustizia Sociale," *La Civilta Cattolica*, 1936, Vol. 1, pp. 353–364; Vol. 2, pp. 111–123, and 186–198.

Bruehl, Charles, *The Pope's Plan for Social Reconstruction* (New York: Devin-Adair Co., 1939).

Cantwell, John E., S.J., "A Fourth Species of Justice," *Social Order*, Vol. 4, No. 6, June, 1954, pp. 272–276.

Cathrein, V., S.J., "Uberfluss und Almosen," *Theologisch-praktische Quartalschrift*, Vol. 82, No. 4, 1929, pp. 674–687.

Corrigan, Jos. W., and O'Toole, G. B. (ed.), *Race: Nation: Person* (New York: Barnes and Noble, 1944).

Cronin, John F., S.S., *Catholic Social Principles* (Milwaukee: The Bruce Publishing Co., 1950).

———— *Economics and Society* (New York: American Book Co., 1939).

———— "Social Exchange Today," *Social Order*, Vol. 1, No. 10, Dec., 1951, pp. 435–439.

Damen, C., C.Ss.R., "De Recto Usu Superfluorum," *Analecta Gregoriana*, Vol. 9, 1935 (Rome: Gregorian University).

Dawson, Christopher, *Beyond Politics* (New York: Sheed and Ward, 1939).

Delos, J. T., O.P., "Le Bien Commun International et Les Enseignements du Saint-Siege," in *Le Desordre de l'Economie Internationale et la Pensee Chretienne, Semaines Sociales de France* (Lille), 1932 (Paris: Gabalda, 1932).

Dempsey, Bernard W., S.J., "The Roots of Business Responsibility," *Harvard Business Review*, Vol. 27, No. 4, July, 1949, pp. 393–404.

Derrick, Michael, *The Portugal of Salazar* (New York: Campion Books Ltd., 1939).

Doolan, Aegidius, O.P., *Order and Law* (Westminster: Newman Press, 1954).

Eberdt, Mary Lois, C.H.M., and Schnepp, Gerald J., S.M., *Industrialism and the Popes* (New York: P. J. Kenedy and Sons, 1953).

Fanfani, Amintore, *Catholicism, Protestantism and Capitalism* (New York: Sheed and Ward, 1935).

Ferree, William, S.M., *The Act of Social Justice* (Dayton: Marianist Publications, 1951).

—— *Introduction to Social Justice* (New York: The Paulist Press, 1948).

George, Gordon, S.J., "The Family Living Wage," *Social Order,* Vol. 1, No. 9, Nov., 1948, p. 385; and Vol. 2, No. 1, Jan., 1949, p. 23.

Gundlach, Gustav, S.J., "Stand und Klasse," *Stimmen der Zeit,* Vol. 117, No. 4, 1929, pp. 284–293.

Hayes, Carleton J., *A Generation of Materialism* (New York: Harper, 1942).

Hyland, Philip, O.P., "The Field of Social Justice," *The Thomist,* Vol. 1, No. 3, Oct., 1939, pp. 295–330.

International Union of Social Studies, *A Code of Social Principles,* trans. from the 2nd French edition (Oxford: The Catholic Social Guild, 1937).

Jarrett, Bede, O.P., *Social Theories of the Middle Ages* (Boston: Little Brown and Co., 1926).

Kelly, Gerald, S.J., "The Common Good and the Socio Economic Order," in *Proceedings* of the 7th Annual Convention of the Catholic Theological Society of America, June, 1952 (New York: Paulist Press), pp. 83–107.

—— "Notes on Moral Theology," *Theological Studies,* Mar., 1950, pp. 38–42.

Kennedy, Paul V., S.J., "Labor's Participation in Management: Ethical Aspects," *Review of Social Economy,* Vol. V, No. 1, June, 1947, pp. 49–59.

Kleinhappl, Johan, S.J., "Der Begriff der 'Justitia Socialis' und das Rundschreiben 'Quadragesimo Anno,' " *Zeitschrift fur Katholische Theologie,* Vol. 58, 1934, pp. 364–390.

Lacroix, Jean, "Justice and Charity," *Theology Digest,* Vol. 2, No. 3, autumn, 1954, pp. 182–185.

Land, Philip, S.J., and Klubertanz, George, S.J., "Practical Reason, Social Fact, and the Vocational Order," *The Modern Schoolman*, Vol. 28, No. 4, May, 1951, pp. 239–266.

Lauer, Quentin, S.J., "Co-management In Germany," *Social Order*, Vol. 1, No. 1, Jan., 1951, pp. 11–22.

Leclercq, Jacques, *Lecons De Droit Naturel*, 5 vols. (Namur: Wesmael-Charlier); Vol. I, *Le Fondement du Droit de la Societe* (1933); Vol. IV, part 2, *Les Droits et Devoirs Individuels: Travail, Propriete* (1937).

Leo XIII, Pope, *Immortale Dei*, encyclical on the Christian Constitution of States, Nov. 1, 1885 (*The Catholic Mind*, Vol. 34, No. 21, Nov. 8, 1936).

———— *Rerum Novarum*, encyclical on the Condition of Labor, May 15, 1891 (Washington, D. C.: N.C.W.C., 1942).

Lopez, Ulpanius, S.J., "Divini Redemptoris — Annotationes," *Periodica de Re Morali*, etc., Vol. 26, 1937, p. 275 (Rome: Gregorian Univ.).

MacDonnell, Joseph, S.J., *An Approach to Social Justice* (St. Louis: Central Bureau Publications, 1937).

Maritain, Jacques, *Man and the State* (Chicago: Univ. of Chicago Press, 1951).

———— "The Natural Law and Human Rights," *The Dublin Review*, Vol. 210, No. 421, Apr., 1942, pp. 116–124.

———— "Religion and Culture," in *Essays in Order*, ed. C. Dawson (New York: Sheed and Ward, 1940).

Messner, J., *Ethics and Facts* (St. Louis: B. Herder Book Co., 1952).

———— *Social Ethics*, trans. J. J. Doherty (St. Louis: B. Herder, 1949).

———— "Soziale Gerechtigkeit," in *Staatslexikon*, Vol. 4, col. 1664–1669 (Freiburg: Herder, 1931).

Michel, V., O.S.B., *Christian Social Reconstruction* (Milwaukee: The Bruce Publishing Co., 1937).

Miller, Raymond J., C.Ss.R., *Forty Years After: Pius XI and the Social Order* (St. Paul: Radio Replies Press, 1947).

Mueller, Franz H., *Heinrich Pesch and His Theory of Christian Solidarism* (St. Paul: The College of St. Thomas, 1941).

———— "Person and Society According to St. Thomas," in *Thomistic Principles in a Catholic School*, by T. Brauer and Others (St. Louis: B. Herder Book Co., 1943), pp. 184–263.

——— "Rejecting Right and Left: Heinrich Pesch and Solidarism," *Thought,* Vol. 26, No. 103, Winter, 1951–1952, p. 485.

Mulcahy, Richard E., S.J., *The Economics of Heinrich Pesch* (New York: Henry Holt and Co., 1952).

Muller, Albert, S.J., *Notes D'Economie Politique,* deuxieme serie, "La Circulation et la Distribution des Biens" (Paris: Editions Spes, 1938).

Munier, J. D., *Some American Approximations to Pius XI's "Industries and Professions"* (Washington: Catholic Univ. Press, 1943).

Nell-Breuning, von, Oswald, S.J., *Reorganization of Social Economy,* English edition by Bernard W. Dempsey, S.J., (Milwaukee: The Bruce Publishing Co., 1936).

——— "Um den Berufstandischen Gedanken," *Stimmen der Zeit,* Vol. 122, No. 1, 1932, pp. 36–52.

——— "Um die 'Berufsstandische Ordnung,'" *Stimmen der Zeit,* Vol. 142, No. 7, 1948, pp. 6–19.

Newman, Jeremiah, *Foundations of Justice* (Cork: Cork Univ. Press, 1954).

Noldin, H., S.J., Schmitt, S.J., *Summa Theologiae Moralis,* Vol. II, *De Praeceptis,* 20th ed. (Innsbruck, 1930).

O'Hanley, J. P., "Social Justice: Meaning — Necessity — Promotion," *Homiletic and Pastoral Review,* Vol. 38, No. 11, Aug., 1938, pp. 1152–1164.

Parsons, Wilfred, S.J., "What Are Vocational Groups?" *Thought,* Vol. 17, No. 66, Sept., 1942, pp. 464–476.

——— *Which Way Democracy?* (New York: Macmillan, 1939).

Pius XI, Pope, *Casti Connubii,* encyclical on Christian Marriage, December 31, 1930 (*The Catholic Mind,* Vol. 29, No. 2, Jan. 22, 1931).

——— *Divini Redemptoris,* encyclical on Atheistic Communism, Mar. 19, 1937 (Oxford: Catholic Social Guild, 1937).

——— *Quadragesimo Anno,* encyclical on Reconstructing the Social Order, May 15, 1931 (Washington: N.C.W.C., 1942).

Pius XII, Pope, "Address to the Delegates to the Catholic International Congresses for Social Study and Social Action," Rome, June 3, 1950, *The Catholic Mind,* Vol. 48, No. 1052, Aug., 1950, p. 507.

——— "Address to the Ninth International Union of Catholic

Employers," Rome, May 7, 1949, *The Catholic Mind,* Vol. 47, No. 1039, July, 1949, p. 445.

——— *Pius XII and Democracy,* Christmas Message of 1944, trans. John B. Harney, C.S.P. (New York: Paulist Press, 1945).

——— *Sertum Laetitiae,* encyclical on Progress and Problems of the American Church, November 1, 1939 (*The Catholic Mind,* Vol. 37, No. 886, Nov. 22, 1939, p. 923).

——— *Summi Pontificatus,* encyclical on the Unity of Human Society, October 20, 1939 (New York: America Press, 1939).

Rommen, Heinrich A., *The State in Catholic Thought* (St. Louis: B. Herder, 1945).

Ryan, John A., *Distributive Justice,* 3rd ed. (New York: Macmillan, 1942).

Schumpeter, Joseph A., *History of Economic Analysis* (New York: Oxford University Press, 1954).

Schuyler, Joseph B., S.J., "Vangheluwe On Social Justice," *Social Order,* Vol. 2, No. 5, May, 1949, p. 203.

Schuyler, Jos. B., S.J., and Carmody, James M., S.J., "Thoughts On Social Justice," *Social Order,* Vol. 2, No. 6, June, 1949, p. 245.

Shields, Leo W., *The History and Meaning of the Term Social Justice* (Notre Dame, Ind., 1941).

Smith, William J., S.J., "The 'Catholic' Viewpoint on Industry Councils," *American Ecclesiastical Review,* Vol. 122, Feb., 1950, pp. 107–120.

Suarez, Francis, S.J., *De Legibus,* ed. C. Berton (Paris: Vives, 1856).

Tiberghien, P., "Comment Inserer dans l'Economie Moderne la Conception Chretienne de la Propriete," in *La Morale Chretienne et les Affaires,* Semaines Sociales de France (Mulhouse) 1931 (Paris: Gabalda).

Timasheff, Nicholas S., and Facey, Paul W., S.J., *Sociology* (Milwaukee: The Bruce Publishing Co., 1949).

Vangheluwe, V., "De Justitia Sociali," *Collationes Brugenses,* Vol. 43, 1947, pp. 309–321, 383–398; 436–448; Vol. 44, 1948, pp. 306–319, 388–395.

——— "De Privato Dominio Proprietatis," *Collationes Brugenses,* Vol. 43, 1947, pp. 99–110.

——— "De Privati Dominii Proprietatis Limitibus," *Collationes Brugenses,* Vol. 43, 1947, pp. 176–183.

Vermeersch, A., S.J., "Soziale Krize und Reformtheorien," *Theologisch-praktische Quartalschrift,* Vol. 82, No. 4, 1929, p. 687.

———— *Theologiae Moralis,* Principia — Responsa — Consilia, 4th ed. (Rome: Gregorian Univ., 1947).

———— *Quaestiones De Justitia,* 2nd ed. (Bruges: Beyaert, 1904).

Viglino, Ugo, I.M.C., "The Social Function of Property and Its Metaphysical Foundation," *Theology Digest,* Vol. 1, No. 3, autumn, 1953, pp. 164–168.

Waffelaert, G. J., *De Justitia,* 2 vols. (Bruges: Beyaert-Storie, 1886).

Ward, Leo R., C.S.C., *Christian Ethics* (St. Louis: B. Herder Book Co., 1952).

Watt, Lewis, S.J., *Capitalism and Morality* (London: Cassell, 1929).

Williams, Melvin, *Catholic Social Thought* (New York: Ronald Press, 1950).

Index